100 Great

EFL Games

Exciting Language Games
for Young Learners

Adrian Bozon

Crazy Chopstick Publications

Contents

Foreword

Students learn best when they are having fun and they rarely have more fun than when they are playing games. Games motivate students and provide invaluable chances to practise and consolidate learning in an enjoyable setting. Even the minority of students who may be slightly passive or resistant to other parts of a lesson can usually be drawn in to take a full part in games and related activities. It follows therefore, that all teachers of English as a Foreign Language should have a healthy and varied repertoire of games at their disposal, particularly if their students are young.

This book aims to provide teachers with a wealth of games and ideas to improve their lessons. A key focus of these games is improving the students' speaking and communicative ability but there are several games for consolidating their reading and writing skills too. There are activities for students of all abilities, ranging from those that have only just learned the alphabet to those who have reached quite an advanced level. While there is not a chapter devoted specifically to games for advanced level students, these students have not been ignored. Several of the game variations are suitable for these students as are the games for all in chapter six. Some games will appeal to young learners while others will be more relevant for older students. A minority of the games will work much better with either a small or large class but most are suitable for all class sizes and also for classes of mixed ability.

Many of the games are ready to go and thus great for teachers in need of some inspiration on the spur of the moment or for those in a hurry or short of preparation time. Others will require a fair amount of preparation but hopefully the results will make the extra effort worthwhile. Variations are offered for every game, while teachers themselves may suddenly find inspiration to make the sort of effective, subtle alterations to the original format that keep the games fresh and the students interested. Do not be afraid to experiment nor be downhearted if new ideas do not come off. Some of the games in this text have suggested target vocabulary or a key question and a range of answers. In many cases this can be easily adapted for the needs of a particular class.

While I anticipate this book will be particularly helpful to relatively inexperienced teachers, I am sure more experienced teachers will also find it a useful source of fresh ideas, either in the form of new games or variations of games they may already know. Additionally, the ideas here should be a highly valuable resource to teachers teaching foreign languages such as French or German in their own countries, whether it be at primary schools, secondary schools or elsewhere. I think particularly of teachers in English primary schools, many of whom have, in recent times, suddenly found themselves thrust into teaching a foreign language.

Whatever your background, I hope this book brings you and your students lots of enjoyment and contributes to good language acquisition. Finally, I would like to thank all the teachers and students at Cheongju Gyoyukdae Buseol Elementary School for making my time there so enjoyable, with a special thank you to Yongpyo Lee for being so helpful and kind.

Adrian Bozon

1

First Day

Guess about the Teacher

A common fear of new teachers, especially those taking their first English language teaching job, is their very first lesson. This is understandable in all cases but even more so if it is the teacher's first job after graduation or first time living abroad. If the teacher has had no formal training in teaching English, it is only natural that these fears will be greater. However, there is no reason why the first day should not be very enjoyable. Most students will be very curious and excited about having a new teacher. Take advantage of this to get off to a good start. There is no essential preparation for this activity but taking some pictures or photos from your own country is generally a good idea.

Method

Ask students to guess various facts about you but do not allow yourself to be pressured into disclosing anything you do not want to. They can guess what country the teacher comes from, the teacher's age, favourite food, animals etc.

Variations

For slightly older students, use photos or pictures as aids, ideally displayed on a TV, computer or large screen in your classroom. Show them photos of the leader, queen, leading sports stars or pop singers from your country. Ask who they are. Also ask the students to tell you about their country.

2

Games for Beginners and Very Young Learners.

Make the Alphabet

Each team needs a set of alphabet cards or magnets and the teacher needs a timer for this simple game.

Method

Divide the students into small teams. The teacher prepares alphabet cards or magnets and mixes them well. Depending on the teacher's preference and number of cards, teams could play separately in a timed game or all at the same time in a speed game. When the teams are ready, the teacher throws a set of letters onto each desk or on the floor. The members of each team must work together and try to find and rearrange the letters alphabetically as quickly as possible. When a team has the letters arranged alphabetically, they must sing a recognized alphabet song. If the teams are playing separately, the teacher stops the timer at the end of the song and the next team has its turn. If the teams are playing at the same time, the first team to finish with the alphabet correctly arranged wins the game.

Variations

If the students are not absolute beginners, challenge them by giving them a few rogue letters in their set. For example if they are doing small letters, add a capital W, U, Z and/or a few others and see if they can work out which letters belong and which do not.

Alphabet Speed Game

This is a good kinesthetic activity to use with very young learners. It is an ideal way to motivate the children at the start of a class. It is also good between tasks to keep the students lively. The class size needs to be twenty-six or less. Thirteen or less is even better as every student can receive at least two letters. Use one piece of large paper for each letter. Clearly distinguish letters that look similar depending on which way up they are held.

Method

Distribute the letter papers randomly between the students. Depending on the class size, some students will often have one more letter than other children. Students start sitting down on the floor or on their chairs. On the floor close together often works well. When the teacher starts the timer, the student with the letter A must stand or jump up quickly, hold the letter above his head, shout, 'A' and sit down again. The student with B then does the same but shouts, 'B'. Continue until the students reach Z then stop the timer. If students go out of order, prompt them and go back to the last correct letter.

When they finish, write the students' time on the board. Except for the first lesson when they are getting used to the activity, only let them try once per lesson and challenge them to improve their best time. Consider giving them a small prize when they manage to do it in thirty seconds or less for the first time and then set a new target for future lessons.

Variations

Instead of a whole class challenge, consider a boys versus girls game with each team going in turn. The fastest team wins. One advantage of this approach is that each student will receive more letters and more opportunities.

Finger Drawing

This is a very simple way to get young learners practising lots of vocabulary quickly, through a series of guesses and answers. No preparation is necessary unless a teacher chooses to make picture cards for team games.

Method

Choose a topic, such as shapes, toys or animals and ask a student to stand up at the front of the classroom. The student does not talk but instead draws an object with his finger in the air. Other students have to try and guess the answer. There are no penalties for wrong responses. If no-one knows, ask the student to draw the same thing again. The student who answers correctly does the next question. Choose a new student if no-one answers. After about three or four questions as a class, split the class into pairs or small groups and let students play among themselves. Students play just for fun without a points system rather than playing competitively.

Variations

Split the class into two teams. One volunteer represents each team per round. Teams play in turns and have a time limit of fifteen or thirty seconds. The teacher shows picture cards to the volunteer one at a time and that student then draws the pictures in the air. Teams score one point per right answer. Multiple guesses are allowed but passes are not. The team with the most points wins each round.

Body Spelling (1)

This is a kinesthetic activity to practise letters or short words. It is good for very young learners.

Method

One person says a letter of the alphabet and specifies whether it should be a capital or small letter. Students must then make that letter with their bodies, using their arms or legs, in whatever way is appropriate. They can stand up or lie down on the ground. Students can make the letters individually or find other students to help complete a letter. Students might pair up to make letters such as V or X. They can get into bigger groups for more complicated letters such as W, S or capital R.

Variations

Split the class into a boys' team and a girls' team and give them short words to make.

The Colour Game

This is a simple kinesthetic game for young learners to practise colours.

Method

After teaching the names of the colours, the teacher gives simple instructions such as, 'Touch something red' and students have to quickly look for something and put a hand or finger on it. Students may stand up and move around the classroom to find something of the appropriate colour.* They can touch anything they want, including books, pictures, stationery and clothes. Students who touch something of the wrong colour are eliminated, as is the slowest student or students to touch the right colour. After

---

* Arrange the classroom so that the students can move quickly, freely and safely.

the first round, consider choosing eliminated students each time to give new instructions. Continue until only one or a few students are left or until all or most common colours have been used.

Variations

Challenge the better students by saying, 'Touch something white except X' or introduce a twister element, giving instructions such as, 'Touch something green with your right hand and something red with your left hand.'

Alternatively, get the students to stay seated and play the game for fun in their table groups, with students taking turns to give instructions.

Place Value

On first thought this game might seem more suited to a maths class but it is also well-suited to an English class as a short activity for practising numbers. Students enjoy the suspense this game can create. Use a massive sponge dice (if available) and a few smaller dice.

Method

For large classes, this game can be played at desks in pairs or small groups. For small classes, one big class game can be played instead. Before starting the game, the teacher or students make up a simple grid for recording the dice score, using tens and units columns. Where the students have higher ability the game could be extended to at least hundreds, tens and units. Hundreds, tens and units generally works well.

The first student or team rolls a dice and then chooses where to put the number. For example if the student rolls a five, he may choose to put it in the tens column. The other student then rolls and decides where to put his own number. If the first student rolls a six on his second turn and puts it in his units column, his final score will be fifty-six for the round. When all students have filled their grids, they read the numbers and the highest score wins the round.

Variations

Play the game in reverse, with the opposition choosing where the number rolled should go.

Memory Game (1)

This is a simple game that is ideal for young learners to practise vocabulary. Attach many pictures or magnets to a whiteboard or prepare slides within a computer file* that can be shown easily on a screen in the classroom.

Method

Show the students lots of related pictures and practise the vocabulary. Next, conceal the pictures in some way, or if that is not practical ask the students to close their eyes and put their head down on the desk. Take one picture away or add a new picture and then allow the students to look again. Sometimes moving all of the other pictures or changing the order around challenges the students more. Students then try to guess what has disappeared or appeared. If a computer is being used, prepare several slides containing subtle changes in advance. There are more options available if using a computer. Instead of taking away or adding items, change the colours of one or two objects and challenge the students to spot the changes.

Variations

For higher level students, present lots of sentences and practise together. As before, conceal the sentences and take a sentence away or add a new one. Alternatively change one or two key words within one or two of the sentences and ask students to find and read the changed sentences. Also a previously correct sentence can be changed into an incorrect sentence e.g. Change a verb to an

---

* Microsoft PowerPoint is one of the best options for this.

incorrect tense. Ask students to spot the mistakes and correct them.

Hopscotch

This activity is a good way to review a topic. Students show their understanding of a topic by reaching the end of the hopscotch grid. It does not necessarily have to be a competitive activity. For this example students practise sentences containing park actions, using 'He's', 'She's' and 'They're' correctly. Prepare pictures or animations of people doing various actions at the park or playground. Mark the classroom floor beforehand in a hopscotch formation using tape or another method.

Method

Students can do the activity individually or one after another in small groups. When a student begins, he or she stands on one leg, looks at the first picture and makes a sentence such as, 'He's swinging', 'She's sliding' or 'They're climbing.' Other students listen and check the answers. If the answer is right, the student moves up to the next box on the hopscotch grid. Continue until the student has given ten right answers and progressed to the end of the grid. Other students then do the same. The teacher can make every student do the same ten answers or may mix answers up and use more than ten.

Variations

This activity has almost endless possibilities as it can be adapted to nearly any topic. If a more competitive version is desired, play timed individual or team games or make two hopscotch grids on either side of the classroom and make the game a race.

Pass the Ball

This is a very simple activity for reviewing a question and answer at the end of a class or the start of the next class. The activity works well with low level students. Each group needs one soft ball.

Method

After discussing previous learning, the teacher chooses one question and one answer and gets the students to listen and repeat briefly. The teacher then puts the students into equal sized teams and gives the first student in each team a soft ball. Student One holds the ball and asks Student Two the target question. When he has finished speaking, he passes the ball to Student Two. Student Two answers, turns to Student Three and asks the same question, again passing the ball on when he finishes speaking. Play continues until the last student asks Student One and Student One answers. If some teams have more students, some students may have two turns. Students always use the same answer.

The teacher gives the students time to practise and then organizes a speed game, timing each team. The fastest team wins.

Variations

Play some music and ask the children to quickly pass the ball around to nearby students without speaking. Switch the music off at random times and the student with the ball stands up. The seated students ask the target question and the standing student answers. Repeat.

Liar Liar Liar!

A minor problem of children asking each other their age in an English classroom is that, generally, all or most students are the same age and hence they only hear one answer. By instructing the students to lie, it varies the activity and makes it much more interesting for the children. It often rouses the children's curiosity for learning how to say big numbers. Prepare an answer sheet for students to record their findings and be sure to tell the students the reason for lying in this game and that, under normal circumstances, lying is not a good thing.

Method

This game follows the same procedure as the Survey Game (see page 150). Students walk around and meet their friends. They ask, "How old are you?" and their friends answer, "I'm _____ years old."

Students should lie instead of saying their true age. The only stipulation is that the students must be able to say the number they choose for their age. They can ask the teacher if they need help saying a number. The teacher may want to practise various numbers before starting the activity. Students record their answers on a worksheet.

Variations

Give students additional challenges such as finding two students the same age as themselves or five students older and/or younger than them.

1 Dog, 2 Dogs, 3 Dogs

The idea for this game is largely based on a matchstick game sometimes played in homes or pubs, and has been adapted for English classes. The object is to practise using singular and plural correctly. Prepare an activity sheet containing approximately thirty small pictures of dogs or any other animal.*

Method

Students usually play in pairs and receive one sheet. Students decide who will play first. The student playing second asks, "How many dogs?" and the other student must answer with, "One dog," "Two dogs" or "Three dogs," concentrating on using singular and plural correctly. After saying an answer, the student crosses off a corresponding number of dogs off the sheet. Question and answer roles are then reversed with the matching number of dogs again crossed off. Continue until all dogs have been crossed off. The student who crosses off the last dog is the winner.

Students have no restrictions as to how many times they may use one, two or three. They are not usually penalized for incorrect use of singular and plural but they should be asked to correct wrong answers on an ongoing basis.

---

* I generally use thirty small pictures but in reality any desired total can be used.

Variations

Prepare a variety of sheets allowing students to play further games with different animals.

Alien Teacher

This is a funny game for young learners to practise asking about body parts and classroom objects.

Method

Students get into pairs and each student receives a piece of A4 paper, folded down the middle. Students sit back-to-back. Give the students two or three minutes to draw their aliens on the left side of the paper. Tell them to decide how many heads, eyes, noses, mouths, ears, arms, hands, legs and feet their alien has. If the students have reasonable ability, make the alien look like a teacher by also specifying two or three classroom objects to draw, such as markers, blackboards, books, rulers or computers.

When the students have finished their pictures, they take it in turns to ask each question to the other student using the structure, "How many _____s does your alien teacher have?" and the answer, "He/She has one/two/three heads/eyes." When students get an answer, they draw what they heard on the right hand side of their paper. When both students have asked every question and finished attempting to draw their partner's alien teacher, students look at each others' pictures to see how well they did.

Variations

This style of activity can also be used to practise prepositions with slightly higher level students. Give the students a basic outline of a classroom or room in a house and some objects to draw. Students then use questions such as, 'Where is the teacher?' or 'Where is the pencil sharpener?' and answers such as, 'He's next to the blackboard' or 'It's on the student's desk.'

Nose, Nose, Nose

This is a very simple children's game for practising body parts, which requires no preparation.

Method

The teacher says four body parts and points to them as he speaks. He will almost always start with, 'Nose, nose, nose...' pointing to his nose each time he says the word and then finally he says a different body part such as ear, mouth or foot. Students must listen and point to each of the body parts the teacher says, usually being nose three times and finishing with one other. If the teacher points to a different body part to the one he says, the students must point to the part he said, not the part he touched. The game may be played competitively or just for fun. If students make a mistake or are too slow to respond during a competitive game, they are out of the game. Start slowly and increase speed if students are difficult to eliminate.

Variations

Increase the difficulty by mixing singular and plural forms, using commands such as, 'Nose, nose, nose, ears' followed by, 'Nose, nose, nose, leg', making the students point to the correct number of ears or other body part to stay in the game.

The Face Game

This is a game for young learners, which is similar to pin the tail on the donkey. It is used for practising face vocabulary and basic directions. This game can be played competitively or just for fun and for practise purposes only. It works best for small classes or when it is played in small groups. Prepare magnets (two eyes, two ears, mouth and nose) and a blindfold. Also draw an outline of a face on the board.

Method

Choose a student to be blindfolded. Put one of the face parts in his hand. He has to guess the part of the face just by touch alone. He scores one point for a right answer. After his guess he stands next to the face on the board and the other students in the group use 'left, right, up, down, stop and put it there' to guide him to the correct place. After finishing one face part, he receives a second part, guesses it again and then continues to follow instructions for where to place it. After doing all six parts (two eyes, two ears, nose and mouth) he scores one point for each part correctly identified plus a score of between zero and four, awarded by the teacher for the accuracy of his placement, making a total of ten points. Continue for other students.

Variations

Instead of a human face, give different numbers of face parts such as one or three eyes and ask the students to make an alien. At the end of the game ask the students to vote for the winner.

Can You Help Me?

This is a simple and fun activity for asking and answering, "Can you help me?" It is ideal for introducing or reviewing a lesson. Prepare lots of small soft balls or other light objects that do not break easily.

Method

Choose two volunteers. The first student asks, "Can you help me?" and gives the other student a ball or other object. If the student gathers and holds the object without dropping it, he or she answers, "Sure", "Sure I can", "Okay" or "No problem." The first student then gives the other student a second ball and asks the same question. If the second student can hold both balls, he or she answers in the same way as before. Play carries on in the same way, getting progressively harder for the second student to hold on to everything. Continue until the second student drops one or more of the objects. When the student finally drops something he or she must answer, "Sorry, I can't." The student then scores points according to how many objects he held before dropping something. Repeat for other students. The student with the most points is the winner.

Variations

Consider introducing a pontoon element into the activity by allowing the students to stick at any stage, gaining all the points up to that point. If they do not stick and proceed to drop one or more objects, they are 'bust' and score nothing.

What's in the Box?

This is a simple guessing game to practise asking, "Is it a/an _____?" It will interest young learners and help lower level students. Before the class seal a few boxes with one object inside each box. The object should be a vocabulary item the students are likely to know.

Method

The game can be played individually or in teams.[*] When playing the game, the teacher walks around the classroom and shakes the box near the students as a hint. Students then have some thinking time before each team gives an answer using, "Is it a _____?" The teacher then answers each team using, "Yes, it is" or "No, it isn't." If all teams are wrong, the teacher asks the students to listen to the box shaking again, giving additional hints if necessary. If students do not answer correctly within three rounds, the teacher opens the box and reveals the answer. The right answers score one point. In special cases, the teacher might allow the students to keep the contents of the box for a right answer.

---

[*] I prefer to use teams so that the students can discuss answers together. I often use teams for most of the game before making the last round individual, with the object being something nice, which I allow the student who gets the right answer to keep.

Variations

Give students complete ownership of the game by asking them to prepare their own boxes in advance. The teacher then simply facilitates as the game progresses.

Who is He?

This is a very simple, short and fun game, which is ideal for larger classes. Students practise asking and answering about people. You will need a blindfold.

Method

One volunteer is chosen and blindfolded. A second volunteer is then chosen and placed in front of the blindfolded student. The remaining students ask, "Who is he/she?" and the blindfolded student must try to identify the student within a short time by touch alone. The student answers with, "He's/She's _____" followed by the name of the student and then takes off the blindfold to check the answer. Usually only one guess is allowed.

Variations

After a few rounds, make the activity funnier and more difficult by putting glasses on the student to be identified, even if he or she does not normally wear glasses. Also consider using wigs if there are any available!

This is my Mother

This is a game for practising talking about family members. It can be played in groups as a class game, using concealed pictures on a large screen, most likely produced on Microsoft PowerPoint, or with covered pictures attached to the class whiteboard. It can also be played individually at desks using smaller cards.

Method

Split the class into six groups or less and produce sets of pictures either on the computer or on a classroom board. Use pictures of a grandmother, grandfather, mother, father, brother and sister. Cover the pictures and mix them up before showing the students. In the case of using a computer, prepare several slides in advance, allowing for the possibility of a few rounds play.

When it is a team's turn, it chooses one of the concealed pictures and the teacher shows which family member it is. The students in the team then introduce the person to the rest of the class. If the team chooses a grandmother picture, it would say, "This is my grandmother," and the other teams reply with, "Nice to meet you," with the first team finishing with, "Nice to meet you too."

Teams score three points for finding a grandparent, two points for a parent and one point for a sibling. The teacher may also sometimes award bonus points to teams who speak with big, clear voices. Play in turns and in the case of multiple rounds, start with a different team each time. In the case of there being less than six teams, just allow each team to choose one picture each round with some pictures remaining unused.

For individual games, put the students into small groups with sets of six cards face down on desks. Proceed in the same way as above, using the same conversations. If students are sat in pairs, they could choose more than one card per round. At the end of the round, students put the cards back on the desk face down, mix them up well and start another round. Points from each round are added together to find a winner.

Variations

Add baby brother and baby sister to the game and use a four, three, two, one point system starting with four for the grandparents, going down to one point for the babies or add great-grandparents with them being worth four points each and the other points following the same format as before. Alternatively, add both great-grandparents and baby siblings, and go down from five points to one point.

Body Spelling (2)

This kinesthetic activity practises basic writing, providing an interesting addition to writing in notebooks.

Method

Students pair up, with one student standing behind the other. The student standing behind writes a letter on the back of the other student with only his finger. The student at the front has to 'feel' the letter and identify it. After answering correctly, both students turn around and change roles. For students of a slightly higher level of English, students can write short words instead of letters.

Variations

In the case of writing letters, instead of the student standing in front saying the answer, he then turns around and writes what he thinks the next letter of the alphabet is on his partner's back.

In the case of writing words, instead of the student standing in front saying the answer, he then turns around and writes what he thinks the word was on his partner's back. The students then compare answers.

Weather Game

This is a simple guessing weather vocabulary game for low level students. It can be developed in interesting ways for slightly higher level students.

Method

Put the students into small groups. Choose a few very famous world cities and before teaching, research the weather for the day of the lesson. Preparing a worksheet for each group to record their answers can be useful. Start by asking the students the weather where they live. Next invite them to guess the weather for that day in the chosen cities. Encourage them to think about whether each city is in a hot or cold area and to consider the time of year. They should only talk in English while discussing their guesses. Before the teacher reveals each answer, each team says their answer out loud. Teams score one point per answer. The teacher may just say the answer but it is probably better to open several windows in advance and reveal the answers on a screen in the classroom via the internet, if available.

Variations

Ask a few volunteers to choose a city of their own for the class to predict and then look the weather up on the internet while they choose their answers.

41

After they have been given the answers, ask students in higher level classes to practise and then present the weather for each city in the style of a television weather person. Give them a map they can add weather pictures to. They could give the weather just for the current day or the activity could be developed by initially asking them to predict the weather, not only for the current day, but also for the next day so that they are able to use sentences in both present tense and future tense e.g. It is sunny in New York today. It will snow tomorrow.

3

Games for Upper Beginners.

Whisper Game

This is a team activity, in which each member of the team must fulfill an equal role for the team to win.

Method

Make teams of equal size and ask each team to stand in a line with all students standing in the same direction, quite close together and facing away from the teacher. At the start of the game, the first student in each team goes to the teacher, who shows a card or whispers something into the students' ears.*

The students then return to their teams and tap the second students on the shoulder. Those students turn around and the first students whisper what they saw or heard. If the next student cannot understand, the first student may repeat the message as many times as is necessary. When the second student thinks he knows the sentence he taps the next student on the shoulder, while the first student sits down facing away from the line. This process continues until the end of the line at which point the last student must go to the teacher and say the answer. If he is the first student to give the right answer, his team wins. If he is wrong, his team loses.

---

* For example, 'It's raining/I can play tennis/I like spaghetti' etc.

Variations

Sometimes the final student can be asked to go to the blackboard and draw the answer or take or touch the right card from a selection of cards attached to the board.

One unconventional but interesting version of this game is to have a question start at one end and passed down the line and when it gets to the last student, the student gets an answer from a worksheet or a teacher and the answer is then passed back down the line in reverse order to the direction the question came from. This can be particularly effective in a team-teaching situation as one teacher can provide the question and the other teacher can provide the answer. An example of an effective question might be, 'How much is the book/pencil case?' with a price answer such as ten pounds or five dollars being returned down the line.

Shouting Game

This is the big brother of Whisper Game. The idea is to speak English in a very big, clear voice.

Method

Make teams of equal size and ask each team to stand in a line with all students standing in the same direction but well spread out. At the start of the game, the teacher specifies a question that each student must ask. Students make their own individual answers rather than repeating other answers. There are many questions that could be used but good ones include, 'What is your telephone number?' and 'What did you do last night?'

The student at the back of each line starts the game. That student calls the name of the student in front and shouts the target question. The next student turns around and shouts an answer before turning around again, shouting the name of the next student in front and asking the question. Play continues in this way all down the line. When play reaches the student at the front of the line, that student shouts the question to the student at the back of the line who then answers. The fastest team wins.

Variations

For teachers who do not mind noisy classrooms, make teams go separately and instead of racing, the team with the biggest and clearest voices win.

Five Friends

This game is ideal for practising greetings. Younger, enthusiastic students enjoy this activity. You will need a stopwatch or other timer.

Method

Choose a volunteer. The volunteer stands up and the other students stay seated. The volunteer runs to five different friends one by one and says, "Nice to meet you," every time. Each friend answers, "Nice to meet you too" and they shake hands. The teacher times how long it takes to meet and greet five friends. After a few volunteers have tried, the fastest student is the winner.

Variations

This activity can be used for many different kinds of sentences or questions. The chosen students can ask each of their friends, 'Do you like pizza?', 'What's your telephone number?', 'What are you scared of?' or any other question that the students have studied. Friends answer in sentences.

The number of friends to ask can easily be changed, with three being a good alternative. Instead of designating a number of friends, a time limit can be imposed, with the winner being the person to ask the most friends within twenty or thirty seconds.

For a more simplified version, the chosen student can just run up to five different students and say, "This is my friend, Tom/This is my friend, John."

47

The 100 Points Job Game

This is a game of luck that gives students chance to learn and practise a number of jobs in English. Prepare a Microsoft PowerPoint computer file, consisting of about ten to fifteen slides of concealed job pictures.

Method

Prepare slides before the lessons. Assuming four teams, choose four different jobs for slide one and copy job images into the slide (This could be reduced to two if there will only be two teams). For example there could be four police officers, seven teachers, five artists and nine scientists. Conceal the pictures and write the job title above each picture. In later slides do the same but change some of the jobs and the number of workers for each slide. As the slides progress, make the activity more unpredictable and exciting by occasionally putting very large numbers behind some boxes such as twenty-two singers and zero behind one or two others! It keeps the game open until the end, allowing teams to make a comeback from a slow start.

After deciding the order of play, the first team chooses one of the jobs and asks, "How many teachers/pianists/artists?" The teacher then reveals the picture and they score one point per worker i.e. seven chefs would score seven points. Play continues in turn, with a new slide and different starting team for each round. The first team to score one hundred points wins the game.

Variations

Give each team one or two wild cards, which they can use to score double points for a round.

Spin the Board

This is a very different way of practising a learning goal, such as asking and answering, 'Where are you?'
Prepare a circular board divided into sections, with each containing a picture or word. Put a pin in the centre with a paper clip for spinning attached to it. Flaps covering each answer are an optional but time consuming extra. They are useful for preventing possible student disputes. Provide a checklist for marking off each answer.

Method

Students pair up and decide who will play first. The first player spins the board and then the other asks, 'Where are you?' The first player then looks at the answer he landed on and makes an answer such as, 'I'm at the park.' The student then checks the answer on his sheet and the students change roles. If a student lands on an answer he has already done, the students ask the question and give the answer again but cannot make an additional mark on the checklist. Play continues until one player has marked off every answer.

Variations

As with many activities, the vocabulary can be easily adapted to suit the needs of a given lesson. For example the spinning board could be used to ask and answer, 'What time is it?' Alternatively the focus could be reading, with a different sport or month to read in each sector of the board.

Alphabet Cheat

This is an adaptation of a popular playing cards game, which goes by various names, some of which are less desirable for a classroom! Although its educational value is higher for lower level students as its main purpose is to practise the alphabet, virtually all students, regardless of their level, will enjoy this activity. Prepare sets of 52 cards. Some sets should contain the first thirteen letters of the alphabet (from A to M, with four cards for each letter) and some sets should contain the second half of the alphabet from N to Z. Only use one set at a time. Ideally for the preservation of the cards, they should be laminated.

The teacher should write the relevant thirteen letters of the alphabet on the whiteboard so the students can refer to them at any time. Before playing the game for the first time, the teacher should demonstrate the game very clearly and slowly to avoid student confusion later on. A good demonstration pays off later.

Method

Three or more players can play this game. Four is an ideal number. At the start of the game, all fifty-two cards are distributed as equally as possible face down. After selecting the order of play, the first player must put one, two, three or four cards face down in the middle of the table, depending on the cards he has. Those cards should all be the same letter. He then declares what he has put down i.e. 'Three L's' or 'Two B's.' If the first player puts down some 'B' letter cards, the next player can either put down between one and four of the same letter (B) or of the letter above (C) or the letter below (A) and declare his cards in the same way as the first player. If the previous letter was A, the next player can put down A, B or go back to M. If the previous letter was M, the next player can put L, M or go to A.* Play continues until one player has no cards left. That player wins.

---

* When playing a game using cards from N to Z, a player can follow a Z with either Z, Y or N. N can be followed with N, O or Z.

If a player does not have any of the three letters that he is eligible to put down (or in some cases even if he does!), he is still obliged to put one or more cards down for one of those letters. In this situation he must 'cheat' or 'lie'. For example, if he needs to play an E, F or G, he can put down a B and a J and say, 'Two F's!' or 'Two G's!' If no-one suspects anything then play continues with the next player. At any time, if a player suspects or knows another player has cheated, he may shout, 'Cheat!' before the following player has played any cards. After a call of, 'Cheat!' the cards that were played by the suspect are turned over and checked. If he was indeed cheating, he must pick up and keep all of the cards on the table. If an incorrect call is made, the accuser must take all of the cards. Play then recommences with the player who was due to play next. He restarts the game with any letter.

Variations

Adding one or two jokers to the pack, which can be used for any letter of the alphabet, opens up a world of possibilities with the potential for five or six of any letter in the pack!

4

Games for Lower Intermediate Level Students.

Cat and Mouse

This game is a highly entertaining way of using direction commands in the classroom. Students love this game and it can get very exciting, especially if the cat misses the mouse by a matter of centimetres. You will need a soft toy mallet or rolled up newspaper and two blindfolds. The classroom may need some rearrangement to provide more open spaces.

Method

Split the class into teams. For a smaller class, two teams should be sufficient but for a bigger class, four teams or more with any two teams playing at once works better. At the start of each game both teams choose one student to be the cat or the mouse. The two students then decide who will be the cat and who will be the mouse, most commonly by using rock-paper-scissors. The two students are then blindfolded and the cat is given a fairly soft weapon such as a rolled up newspaper to try and hit the mouse with. The teacher moves the students apart and normally makes them face in opposite directions at the start of the game. The game time is usually one minute.

When the game starts, each team must give directions to their blindfolded friend. They can use instructions such as go straight, turn left, turn right, turn around, stop, faster, turn left a little bit and so on. The cat's team must try to guide their chosen student towards the mouse, while the mouse's team must try to keep away from the cat. Finally, if the cat is very near the mouse, his team shouts, 'Hit!' and the cat can swing his mallet to where he thinks the mouse is. If he hits, he wins. If he misses, he may try again. However, after the third miss, the mouse is deemed to be the winner. If the one minute runs out and the mouse has not been caught, he wins the game.

Variations

If you are team-teaching, one good alternative is to blindfold the teachers for one game and get the male students to guide one teacher and the female students to guide the other teacher. This works well as a review activity at the beginning of the next lesson.

The Apple Game

In this activity, students are motivated to use their knowledge of directions to recreate a famous story. You will need an apple (real or improvised), a soft ball and a blindfold.

Method

Choose one student to be an archer and one to be his son. Blindfold the archer and gently turn him around a few times so that he loses his bearings. Give him a soft ball. Situate the other student a few metres away, with the apple placed on his head, or held gently if it will not balance. The archer holds his hand up with the ball. Another student or a group guides the archer using vocabulary such as up, down, left, right, turn around, higher, lower and finally, 'Throw!'

Give the archer three chances to hit the apple, keeping the blindfold on between unsuccessful attempts. Give brief feedback after an unsuccessful attempt. After a successful attempt or three failures, change students.

Variations

Play a timed game. How many apples can the archer hit within one minute?

Mosquito Game

This game offers a fast and entertaining way for students to practise reading targeted vocabulary. The killing mosquitoes concept is particularly appealing to young male students. You will need a fly-swatter (real or improvised) and you should write a selection of words on the blackboard or whiteboard.

Method

The most common method is to choose a student and give him a time limit of around twenty seconds. The student stands next to the board with the swatter in his hands. When the time starts, the teacher says a word and then the student must swat the word as quickly as possible. As soon as the student successfully swats one word, he scores one point and the teacher says another word. It is acceptable to repeat words. In some cases, the teacher can choose other students to call the words instead of the teacher. When the time is over, the teacher gives the student his total score and then invites other students to try and beat the current leading score.

Usually no penalty is given for swatting the wrong word and students are free to try swatting another answer for the same word with just the inconvenience of using up more time but if the teacher feels that students are not reading the words carefully enough, or are guessing, he could skip on to the next word, or even introduce a one point penalty for a wrong answer. This idea has merit for students of good ability who are studying a number of similar words.

Variations

Probably the simplest alternative is for the teacher to time how long it takes each student to hit a specified number of words.

Another option is for two or more students to play the game at the same time. Each student stands an equal distance from the board, armed with a swatter, and then when the teacher calls a word the students must try to hit the word as quickly as possible. The first student to swat the right word scores a point. Either the students just do one word and then change with other students or they play up to a predetermined number of points.

I'm Taller than You

This is another game where students stand in a line. They practise saying sentences with the word 'than'.

Method

Make teams of equal size. Boys versus Girls works well when student numbers allow. Ask the teams to stand in a line from the tallest student to the shortest student. Students should face the back of the student immediately shorter than themselves. When the teacher starts the game, the first student in each team taps the second student on the shoulder and in a clearly audible voice says, "I'm taller than you." The second student then does the same to the third student. Play continues down the line until the final student (the shortest student) who has to run to the first student and shout, "I'm taller than you!" while jumping up and down to look taller than the first student. The fastest team wins.

Variations

After the first game, it is time for the rematch! Students stand in the same lines but everyone turns around and play starts at the other end of the line. This time the students tap the person in front and say, "I'm shorter than you." When play reaches the front of the line, the first student runs to the back, crouches next to the shortest student and shouts, "I'm shorter than you!"

Code Game

Students have to crack a word or sentence code quickly to win a round or game. The activity is suitable for classes large or small and the challenge is usually enjoyed by all. Teachers need to prepare a code grid for easy reference, either on a handout or on a board or screen. Codes to the game words need preparing before the class.

Method

Students have a grid as a visual aid. Usually a=1, b=2, c=3 and so on although in theory the teacher could allocate any letter to any number from one to twenty-six. If the word for the round is 'bad' the teacher calls out, '2, 1, 4' and students have to quickly convert the numbers to letters on their paper. Students put their hands up when they have written the word down and are satisfied they have the right word, having checked the spelling. The teacher should not choose students who raise their hands before they finish writing the word on their paper. The teacher asks the first student for the answer and gives a point or other reward for a good answer. If the second word is 'ate' the teacher calls out, '1, 20, 5.' The game continues until every word the teacher prepared has been completed.

Variations

Make the game more student-centred by giving the students the grid and asking them to make the codes. Each student then reads one code and they can solve each other's words.

One Point, Two Points

This activity requires students to ask many questions. As the game progresses, students tend to become increasingly imaginative in order to earn more points.

Method

The teacher gives the students a particular question structure such as, 'Can you _____?'

If the teacher answers positively (i.e. 'Yes, I can'), the team or student that asked the question only scores one point. However, if the teacher answers negatively (i.e. 'No, I can't'), the team or student that asked the question scores two points. The team with the most points at the end wins.

Variations

Many different question structures can be used such as, 'Do you like _____?' followed by foods, animals, etc. Another good one is, 'Did you _____ during the vacation?'

Although it is more common to award two points for a negative response and one point for a positive, the points system can be reversed if desired.

One More Card?

This is another activity which requires students to ask many questions. As a turn progresses the team has to decide whether to risk everything in pursuit of a bigger score. Prepare food or telephone number cards in advance.

Method

The teacher prepares a set of food cards. Six different food cards each produced four or five times is a good number. Thoroughly shuffle the cards before starting the game. At the start of a team's turn, the teacher puts one card on the board, face up. Other teams ask, "Do you want some more?" and the team whose turn it is must decide whether to play or stick. If they want to stick, they say, "No, thank you" and the number of cards already on the board becomes their score. If they want to play, they say, "Yes, please" and the teacher puts the next card in the pack on the board. If the card is a new food, they are safe and they can take another card or stick after the other students have asked the question again. If the new card duplicates one already on the board, they are bust and score zero for the round or game.

Variations

This game can also be used when the students are studying telephone numbers. This time, the teacher makes many cards with the same telephone number on and a much smaller number of cards with alternative numbers. The game always starts with the most common number card on the board. If a team wants to take another card it asks, "Is this _____?" adding the main telephone number. The teacher then reveals the next card. If it is the same number, the teacher replies, "Yes, speaking," but if it is a different number, the teacher replies, "Sorry, wrong number." If the students get a wrong number they lose all of their points for the round.

Baseball

This is an interesting way to practise a chosen question and answer related to the current lesson. Many children like the link to baseball and enjoy the competitive element. You will need a soft ball, timer and scoreboard.

Method

After practising the key question of the lesson and various answers, the students are split into groups of five. Teams take it in turns to play. When it is a team's turn they spread around the classroom in a kind of diamond formation to represent each base with a pitcher in the centre.

When everyone is ready, the teacher starts a timer and the pitcher asks the question before throwing the soft ball to where the striker would normally be in baseball. That student catches the ball and answers the question. He then asks the question to the student on the first base and throws the ball. The student on first base catches the ball, answers the question and then throws it on to the next student. Play continues until the student on third base has answered the question. At this point, instead of throwing the ball to the final base (where the first student to answer the question stands) the student on third base asks the question and throws the ball back to the pitcher who is the only student up to that point not to have answered the question. When the pitcher answers the question, the teacher stops the timer.

If the ball is dropped at any point, the student it was aimed at must retrieve it and return to the relevant base before continuing with play.

In theory the game could be played only once by each team but if at all possible, it is better for every team to play at least twice with each round being called an innings hence the baseball concept.

After each team's turn the teacher records the time on a scoreboard, that is visible to students. After all innings have been completed, the teacher totals the times and the team that uses the least time overall wins the game.

Variations

Normally the teacher records each time on the board as soon a team's turn has finished. However, a teacher can build up suspense by holding back all the times until the end of the game. Time penalties can also be added for failing to catch the ball or for wayward throws.

Five in a Row

This game combines reading with strategy. Prepare a grid of words, with each square containing a word. The words might be general, from the book the students are studying, or words that are challenging for students to read. Each square has a different word but if the students are studying very specific vocabulary such as months, words can be repeated several times and the grid squares labelled i.e. A1 February, A2 December. The grid size varies but eight squares by eight is ideal.

Method

Students form pairs. After practising the game words together as a class, students choose who will start. On each turn, students must read the word they want and then initial it or mark it in some way. Play alternates. The first student to highlight five words in a row in any direction, including diagonally, wins the game.

Variations

Do a beat the teacher challenge. Can the students get five in a row before the teacher?

Edge to Edge

This game focuses on reading and also involves an element of strategy. Before the class, prepare eight by eight grids with one word in each box.

Method

Students play in pairs. Before starting the game, students decide who will go first. They also decide which player will try to get from top to bottom and which player will try to get from left to right. The first student chooses any square on the board and reads the word and clearly marks it off. The second student then chooses a different word and marks it off, clearly distinguishing it from the other student's words. Play continues in turn.

Although students can choose any word at any time, the ultimate aim is to make a completely connected line from one edge of the board to the other (either left to right or top to bottom as determined before the game). Students may use diagonals as part of their complete connected line in order to win the game. Students may play strategically to try and block their opponent. Only one player may mark a particular box. The first player to get a completely connected line from one edge to the other wins.

Variations

Make the game more speaking focused. Instead of just reading one word, prepare a set of answers to a particular question with one answer per box and then the students ask and answer. One possibility is to put a different year in each box. One student asks, "When was he/she born?" and the other student chooses a year and says an answer such as, "He was born in 1962." Play continues in exactly the same way as the simpler reading version of the game. If the number of answers to a particular question are limited, it is fine to have the same answer in more than one box.

Four Knights

This is another two player game, inspired by chess. It combines reading with an element of strategy. Before the class, prepare six by six grids with one word in each box. If you have any available, provide the students with knights from chess sets or black and white counters. If these are not available, students can use any alternatives such as erasers or small pencil sharpeners.

Before the students play the game for the first time, they will need some very clear illustrations as to how knights move in chess. Several students will not know how to play chess. Often students will start their first game uncertainly but quickly pick up the method and start to enjoy the game, with the boys often particularly interested.

Method

At the beginning of the game, students decide who will be white and who will be black. White moves first. The knights start on their regular chess starting squares (one across from each corner). The starting squares are not marked. The first student moves one of his knights following the rules of chess,* reads the word on the square he lands on and clearly marks the square off, ideally using a colour pen or crayon. The other student does the same for one of his own knights and play continues in turns, reading the words each time. Students can move either knight on any given turn. Students cannot move to any square that has already been marked by either player.

The game method differs to chess in that students may not capture the opponent's knights. Instead the aim is to trap the knights. If one player moves one of his knights somewhere that leaves one of the opponent's knights with no unmarked squares to move to, the player takes the trapped knight off the board. Alternatively, if a player makes a mistake and manages to move somewhere that

---

* A knight may move two squares vertically and one horizontally or two squares horizontally and one vertically in any direction.

traps his own knight, his knight is taken off the board immediately. As the game progresses and many squares get marked, players will inevitably end up with nowhere to go. The first player to lose both knights loses the game.

Variations

Although a six by six grid is the recommended size, bigger grids such as a standard eight by eight chess board are fine if there is enough time available for the activity. The game can be made more speaking focussed in much the same way as in the Edge to Edge game (see page 66). One possible question is, 'Where did you go in the vacation?' with every box containing a city or country name. Therefore answers could be, 'I went to China' or 'I went to Seoul.'

50 Points Daily Habits Game

This is an interesting way to practise talking about daily habits, combining speaking with strategy. Prepare a check sheet containing a table with all twelve hourly times from one o'clock to twelve o'clock.

Method

Students play in pairs and receive one check sheet. Students decide who will play first. Students make sentences in turn, using the structure, "I _____ at _____."

If the first student says, 'I get up at seven,' seven is checked off and cannot be used again in the game. The running total is seven. The second student then makes a sentence such as, 'I eat lunch at one.' Following this, one is checked off and one is added to seven to make a running total of eight. Play continues in turns until one student's answer takes the total to or past fifty. The student who reaches fifty is the game winner.

All answers should be on the hour (at 7:00, seven o'clock etc.). Minutes are not used in this game. If students cannot make a sentence, they are allowed to receive help.

Variations

Play in reverse, with the student who takes the score to or past fifty losing the game. Alternatively only allow exactly fifty points to win the game and if the running total exceeds fifty, the game is drawn and students play again.

Memory Game (2)

This is a game for practising future tense in which, students use a simple sentence to practise many answers.

The longer the game goes on without a mistake, the more excited the students become.

Method

The game is usually played individually. Depending on class size, the teacher may organize a whole class game or group games.

After practising the sentence structures, "I will _____" and "Jinsu/Michael will _____", the students can begin the game. Students must correctly use the sentences to talk about their plans for the next vacation.

The first student says a sentence and then the next student must say the first student's name and plan and then add an answer, with later students continuing. For example, Student One says, 'I will go to Seoul.' Student Two says, 'Jinsu will go to Seoul and I will study English.' Student Three says, 'Jinsu will go to Seoul, Tony will study English and I will practise the piano.' If all students answer without a mistake, return to Student One who recites all the previous answers and then adds a second answer of his own.

Variations

Play the game after a vacation, using past tense, e.g. 'Sangyu visited England and I watched TV.'

Memory Game (3)

In this game students use luck and sometimes good memory later in the game to practise a target question such as, 'What do you want to do?' and a range of answers. Prepare twelve picture or word cards with six different answer cards produced twice each.

Method

The game is usually played in pairs but playing with more students is possible. The cards are placed on the desk faced down. Practise the game question and all possible answers as determined by what is on the cards.

The student not playing first asks the other student, "What do you want to do?" and that student must guess what is on the top card by answering, "I want to _____." If the student answers correctly, he keeps the card. If the student is wrong, the card is placed at the bottom of the pack. Students may try to remember the cards at the bottom for later. Play rotates and continues until students have successfully guessed every card or until time runs out. The student with the most cards wins.

Variations

The number of cards can vary, such as ten or sixteen but try not to have too many different answers. The game and cards can be easily adapted to different vocabulary such as, 'What are you doing?' or 'What do you want for dinner?'

Memory Game (4)

This is another memory game that gets the students really concentrating and reading lots of words. Prepare a large piece of paper full of words, a computer file that can be shown easily on a screen or TV in the classroom, or a projector for showing the words.

Method

This game can be played in pairs or teams but individually is perhaps the best approach. Each student or team receives an answer paper containing all the words the students will see. Usually about five or six words related to a recent topic such as weather words or the names of bugs is effective. Any number of rounds is possible but two rounds works well, with the first round containing the words a relatively small number of times each and then a more difficult second round in which the words are repeated several times each, often drawing gasps when the students first see them!

When the students are ready to start, the teacher reveals the words and the students have to silently try to read and count how many times they can see each word. They should not write while the words are displayed. After a short time (maybe between twenty and forty seconds depending on the number of words) the words are taken away and the students write how many times they think they saw each word, guessing when they are not sure. Repeat for any additional rounds and then give the answers. The student with the most right answers is the winner. Finish by showing the students the word collections one more time and asking all the students to read the words together.

Variations

If the class size is small enough for the students to be split into three or four smallish teams, extend the activity to a writing section. Instead of the teacher preparing the word collections, give each team a few minutes to clearly write their own words using colour pens. Then play the reading game as above, with the team whose words are being used sitting out for the round, rejoining when the next team's words are used.

The Shopping Game

Shopping is a topic that offers a wealth of role-play and game options for students of most levels. Students respond well to the real-life stimulus. For this activity, they need shopping lists, two dice per pair of students with paper money being an optional extra.

Method

Students are paired up and each pair receives a pre-prepared shopping list. This could contain a list or pictures of fruits, vegetables, toys, stationery or other items. There are two additional columns, one for each student. Student One looks at the first item and asks for example, 'How much are the apples?' Student Two rolls two dice, and answers, 'They're X Pounds/Dollars/Euros,' according to the total dice score.

Student One writes the price on the shopping list in his column. Roles are then reversed. Student Two asks, 'How much are the apples?' Student One rolls the dice and answers, and finally Student Two records the price in his column. The process continues until each student has asked and answered for every item. The prices are then added together for each student. The student with the lowest total wins, i.e. the student that was able to buy the items for the cheapest price.

Variations

One possibility is for the customer, in the case of the shopkeeper or clerk rolling a double six, to say, 'It's too expensive,' and not buy the item (scoring no points for the round) or make the shopkeeper or clerk roll again to get a discount. Both are likely to be a significant advantage at the end of the game.

Instead of adding two dice to give a price, introduce students to dollars and cents, pounds and pence etc. Roll one dice for the price in dollars and then roll the second dice, add a zero on to the number and make a price in cents so that the students give answers such as, 'It's four dollars and twenty cents' or 'It's five dollars and fifty cents.'

Make higher level students think about grammar by including both items that are sold singularly, and those sold in bulk such as a melon versus bananas; How much is the melon? It's eight pounds. How much are the bananas? They're three pounds.

Many students like to actually give 'money' when they 'buy' something. This adds realism to the situations and dialogues. If the students play with paper money and plastic coins, teach them to say, 'Here's your change.'

It's in the Box

This is a fun activity for practising prepositions, which gets students active and is particularly popular with male students. Before starting, draw a big picture of a box on the classroom whiteboard or blackboard. Prepare something that sticks to a white or blackboard.

Method

After the teacher draws a box, students take it in turns to throw something sticky at the board. If the object misses the board, hits the board but outside the box or hits the board but does not stick, extra chances can be given at the teacher's discretion. If the object sticks, the other students ask, "Where is the _____?" and the student who threw the ball or other object answers, "It is in/on/under the box."

If the students are playing in teams, one point is usually awarded for landing in the box (the biggest section) and making a sentence. Two and three points are scored for landing on and under the box respectively. Scoring systems or incentives may vary for individual games.

Variations

Further motivate the students by drawing a very small area on the box, for which the students will receive a special bonus such as more points, a sticker or candy if they hit the target.

The Magician Game

This is an imaginative way to make students practise prepositions. Students love the chance to try and fool their friends or even act like a wizard. They will need something small to hide, something to hide it in, on or under, and something to conceal it.*

Method

Students are divided into small groups and take it in turns to make the questions. When it is a student's turn, he puts the eraser and cup inside the bag and then tries to fool the other students. The student must put the eraser in, on or under the cup as the other students watch very carefully to try and work out where it is. When the student has finished, he asks, "Where is the eraser?" and the other students each guess using, "It's in/on/under the cup." More than one student can give the same answer. When every student has made a sentence, the answer is revealed and the next student makes a new question.

---

* I always use erasers, paper cups and opaque bags. There are many acceptable alternatives. For young students, teachers could also consider using magic wands and teaching the students how to say, 'Abracadabra.'

78

Variations

The students enjoy playing the game just for fun and seeing whether or not they get the right answers. It is not usually played competitively. If desired, students can score one point for each right answer with the most points winning.

The Kitchen Game

This activity practises listening skills related to kitchenware. Prepare a number of kitchenware items including, but not limited to, knives, forks, spoons, chopsticks, cups, saucers and bowls. Due to the number of items needed, it is often better to play this game with smaller classes.

Method

A number of students sit together with various kitchenware arranged identically in front of them. The teacher or selected volunteer then gives a series of instructions using, 'pick up', 'put down', 'wash', 'dry' and 'put away'. For example the teacher may say, 'Pick up the spoon,' 'Put down the fork,' 'Dry the bowl,' 'Wash the cup,' 'Put away the plate,' 'Don't pick up the knife, pick up the chopsticks' or 'Don't put down the bowl and pick up the saucer.' Students listen and do or in the case of 'wash' or 'dry' they act the instructions out. Students do not put down an object they have already picked up unless they receive a specific instruction to do so, even if it means holding multiple objects.

Each round usually starts slowly with the instructions getting faster and faster until a student makes a mistake. Usually this game is just played for fun and everyone has a laugh when someone makes a mistake.

Variations

Make the game more confusing and challenging by giving instructions such as, 'Pick up the cup with your left/right hand.' For larger classes, consider using large picture cards instead of actual utensils so that more students can be involved at one time.

Can I Have Some Juice?

This is a fun and versatile game, which allows the students to do a lot of speaking in a short time. In this case they practise how to ask for, give and receive foods and drinks. Prepare a worksheet containing eighteen small pictures of various foods and drinks with a bigger, empty three by three grid in the middle.

Method

Students work in pairs and each person receives a separate but identical worksheet. Students use a customer and waiter dialogue to try and fill their grid. At the start, students look at the first picture and both students in the pair speak at the same time. If the picture is of a pizza, the students ask, "Can I have some pizza?" and then immediately proceed to a game of rock, paper, scissors. The loser says, "Sure, here you are," the winner says, "Thank you" and finally the loser says, "You're welcome."

After finishing the dialogue, the winner draws or writes the food anywhere in his grid. Play continues for the next picture with students inserting the new food or drink into the dialogue. The first student to fill all nine squares in the grid is the winner.

Variations

Ask the losers to fill their grids by using the remaining foods and drinks and then progress on to a bingo game.

Put On, Take Off

This game provides a good way for students to practise understanding expressions about clothes in a practical way. There are various amusing possibilities. Prepare cut-out pictures of clothes and an outline of a body for every student.

Method

Each student receives a body outline and pictures of clothes. The teacher or selected students then give a series of instructions using the expressions, "Put on your _____" and "Take off your _____." Students try to correctly follow the instructions.

The objective can be simply to get the figure dressed or undressed correctly or speed games are possible. Doing the activity without a competitive element is also fine, especially if the students are having fun. Amuse young students by putting photos of teachers on the heads of the figures and then getting the students to dress them inappropriately such as saying, "Put on your dress!" for a male teacher.

Variations

For a highly motivating start to the lesson, bring in some of your biggest, baggiest, longest clothes and then choose one of the students, ideally one of the smallest and shortest in the class. If your students are young, you will probably make some of them laugh a lot by saying, "Put on your _____," one by one until the student is virtually covered by the oversized clothes.

Find the Animals

This is a fun game for practising prepositions, which works very well in big classrooms. However, students may well scatter things around in their enthusiasm so make sure they clear up any mess they make afterwards! Hide animal pictures, cards or magnets around the classroom before the students arrive.

Method

Start by introducing a fictional story about a local farmer's animals escaping and coming to hide in the English classroom. Ask the students to help find the animals. Give the students a handout to note where all the animals are.

Students have to look around the classroom and try and find the animals. It can be completed either individually or in small groups. When the students spot an animal they record their findings in a relevant box, writing sentences such as, 'The cow is under Minsu's desk,' 'The pig is next to the computer keyboard,' 'The spider is in the dictionary' and 'The sheep is behind the clock'. Clearly state that when students find animals they should not move them or shout anything like, 'The pig is over here!' Continue the activity until one team has found all of the animals or a specified time limit has elapsed.

Variations

Change themes. For example, say a very bad man stole many things from a stationery store and then hid them in our classroom because he heard the police were looking for them or say Santa put next year's Christmas presents in our classroom for safekeeping but now he cannot remember where he put them. Students search and record their findings using the same method as before.

The Calendar Game

This is an activity that practises both months and days, and attracts enthusiasm from younger learners. Prepare and photocopy a calendar for the year condensed into one or two pages.*

Method

Each student receives a calendar handout. Students ask the teacher, "What's the date?" and the teacher answers,

---

* There are several sites on the internet with such calendars or it is fairly simple to make one of your own.

"September 7th/November 11th" etc. and the students have to search for the date and see what day of the week it is. They put their hands up and if chosen by the teacher, answer, "It's Monday" or "It's Friday." If the game is being played competitively, the teacher will usually choose the student who raises his hand first to answer. If the activity is being used just for practise, then the teacher can ask anyone. Students must answer as soon as the teacher chooses them or lose their chance.*

Variations

Choose one student to stand up each time. All other students ask, "When is your birthday?" and the student answers, "My birthday is June 2nd/July 11th" etc. The students quickly search and answer, "It's on Monday/Friday this year."

Clock Game

This fun game practises listening skills related to the time. It offers variety and gets the students moving. You will need one clock per two students. Clocks need to have easily movable hands, maybe making use of drawing pins.

---

* Without this stipulation some students will raise their hands first and then quickly search for the answer thus denying a faster student who truly found the answer first.

Method

Put the students into pairs. One student in each pair has a clock. The teacher says a sentence such as, 'I play tennis at 4:20' or 'I eat breakfast at 7:30' and the student with the clock quickly adjusts the time and holds the finished clock above his head, while his partner does the appropriate action i.e. playing tennis or eating. The first pair to have the correct time and action wins the round and earns a point, sticker or other small reward. Continue for a few rounds, with the students switching roles and alternating between making the time and doing the actions. After one or two teacher-led sentences, choose volunteers to make their own sentences or split the class into groups and give students lots of chances to practise all of the roles, including speaking.

Variations

If clocks are unavailable, ask students to make a body clock to show the time for each sentence i.e. using one arm to represent the time in hours and the other arm for minutes.

For students of lower ability, do a simple body clock activity with one person saying a time and all of the other students making the answer.

What's the Time, Mr Wolf?

This is a nice game to finish off lessons about the time. There are also, 'What's the time, Mr Wolf?' songs on the internet to supplement lessons about time.

Method

The teacher chooses one student to be Mr Wolf and a few others, who will try to escape from the wolf. Mr Wolf stands on one side of the classroom and the other students stand on the opposite side of the classroom. Mr Wolf stands with his back to the other students.

The students ask, "What time is it?" and the wolf answers with any time, such as, "It's seven o'clock." The students take one step forward after each answer from the wolf. Questions and answers continue until the students are close to Mr Wolf. Finally, one time at Mr Wolf's choice, instead of answering with X o'clock, he says loudly, "It's lunch time!" and turns around. He then tries to tap or catch one or more students while the students also turn away and have to quickly try and get back to their original starting position before getting caught.

The students trying to escape can be a team, and if any of them get caught, Mr Wolf wins, or it can be an individual game, with all of the students who escape winning and all of the students that get caught losing.

Variations

Use the same procedure but adapt the vocabulary relevant to the topic being studied. For example if they are studying animals and food, change Mr Wolf to a bird. The other students become bugs. The bugs ask, "What do birds eat?" and the bird answers, "Birds eat fruit." Continue for seeds, berries, worms and others, repeating answers if necessary. When the bugs are close to the bird, the bird can answer the question with, "Birds eat bugs!" and the chase begins!

Mouse in the Clock

This is another fun activity for practising asking and answering the time. Ideally the classroom needs a big whiteboard that is not attached to a wall. Prepare a couple of fairly large-sized pictures of a mouse, either drawn or printed from a computer, laminate them or stick them to card and then cut around them. If possible, attach them to the end of sticks of some sort.

Method

Set a background for the game by teaching the children the rhyme, 'Hickory, Dickory Dock'. Explain that the mouse is now in the clock, which is the whiteboard. Mark from one to twelve o'clock at appropriate sections around the outside of the whiteboard. Choose one or two volunteers to stand behind the whiteboard and be the mice. Choose another student to stand up and play the game. Give the student something such as a rolled up newspaper to hit/swipe/kill the mice with.

The student has a time limit of thirty seconds to hit as many mice as possible. When the teacher starts the timer, all of the seated students ask in a big voice, "What time is it?" and one of the students behind the whiteboard moves his stick to temporarily reveal a mouse slightly above, below or to the side of the board. The student playing the game must try to swipe the mouse as quickly as possible. If he makes contact with the mouse, he then answers, "It is 'X' o'clock," depending on the position of the mouse. For example, if the mouse came up at the centre of the board, he would answer, "It's twelve o'clock."

If the student does not swipe the mouse within approximately two seconds, the student holding it behind the board pulls it back behind the board again. After a mouse has been withdrawn or in the case of the student successfully swiping the mouse and giving a right answer, the seated students then repeat, "What time is it?" and play continues in the same way as above. If the student swipes the mouse but says the wrong time or cannot answer, he does not score a point but all correct responses within the time limit earn one point. Continue until the time runs out and then choose new students to control and swipe the mice.

Variations

Increase the time limit to forty-five seconds or a minute and have teams try to hit the mice, with the students in a team taking it in turns.

Extend the vocabulary by clearly marking A.M. and P.M. on the mice and making students say answers such as, 'It's 7 A.M.' or 'It's 6 P.M.' Alternatively, make four mice and clearly mark them with pictures such as the moon or sunrise and ask the students to answer with sentences like, 'It's eight o'clock in the morning', 'It's two o'clock in the afternoon', 'It's seven o'clock in the evening' or 'It's ten o'clock at night.' One final possibility is to ask the students to make additional sentences for each time. Examples include, 'It's eight o'clock. It's time for school' or 'It's ten o'clock. It's time for bed.'

Pairs

This is a simple activity for practising vocabulary and reading skills. Prepare sets of cards, half of which have pictures on and half of which, have the corresponding words on. Alternatively, present the activity on a computer.

Method

Students play either individually or in small teams. Cards are laid face down in two sections. On one side, there are picture cards and on the other side there are word cards. In turns, students take a card from the picture section and say what the picture is and then take another card from the word section and read the word. If the picture and word match, the student keeps the pair. If they do not match, the cards are replaced face down in the same position. If students cannot say what a picture is or cannot read some of the cards, the other students should be encouraged to help them, rather than penalizing the student in some way. The student or team with the most pairs wins.

Variations

Use this activity for practising past tense. On one side have present tense word cards and then the students have to find the word in its past tense form on the other side.

If there is plenty of time, give students complete ownership of the activity by asking them to make their own pairs games, using any relevant English words and pictures on their cards.

Find Your Friend

This is a simple kinesthetic activity for practising making suggestions. Students of most ability levels should be able to participate. Prepare enough picture or words cards for one per student.

Method

Every student receives one picture card or word card. Students always keep their card a secret until they find a student with the same card. Cards could include pictures of tennis, computer games, studying children etc. Students stand up and walk around the classroom, meeting their friends. When they see another student they refer to their card and make a suggestion such as, 'Let's play tennis.' If the other student also has a tennis card, he replies, "Sure" or "Sounds good." The students then sit down together at a designated spot within the classroom. If he has a different card such as listening to music, he replies, "Sorry, I can't" and they both separate and look for new students to ask.

Continue for a set time or until a set number of students have found a suitable partner.

Variations

The activity can be adapted for other vocabulary. One example is, "Can you X?" replying with, "Yes, I can," for the same card or "No, I can't," for a different card. Another possibility is to give the students food cards. Students ask, "Do you like X?" and the other student replies, "Yes, I do," for the same card or "No, I don't," for a different card.

Whose Book is This?

This is a good activity to use in a co-teaching classroom but it is also perfectly possible with just one teacher. Students combine intuition and luck. Prepare a selection of two peoples' personal belongings, mixed up in one or more bags or boxes.

Method

In a co-teaching situation each teacher brings some belongings, typically between six and eight. If there is only one teacher, it can be good to choose two students to take some things to the teacher for mixing before the lesson. At the start of the game every student stands up. One of the teachers (or one of the students if two students bring things) takes the first object out of the bag and briefly describes it if it is not obvious (such as a ticket, card or particular kind of book). Students use their knowledge of the teachers to answer or guess. If they think the item belongs to Teacher A, they put their hands on their head. If they think the item belongs to Teacher B, they fold their arms. When everyone has chosen, all the students ask with a big voice, "Whose _____ is that?" and one of the teachers answer, "It's mine" or "It's not mine."

Students with the wrong answer are out and must sit down although they continue to ask the question for the later objects. The teacher then reveals the second object from the bag and play continues in the same way until only one student remains or until every item in the bag has been revealed. Putting the belongings into two bags (one bag for each teacher or each student volunteer) and playing twice is recommended to give a second chance to students eliminated on the first question. Teachers can also use objects such as glasses and keys to make the students think about grammar (Whose glasses are those? They're mine.).

Variations

Choose one student to briefly go out of the classroom. While the student is outside, take something from one of the other students (either a simple classroom object or, more interestingly, something the student has brought to school especially for the class). When the student returns, give him the object and he has to try and find the owner by walking up to various students and asking, "Whose _____ is this?" When a student is asked, he must answer in the same way as before ("It's mine" or "It's not mine."). Continue until he finds the owner of the object or until he has used up a specified number of wrong guesses.

Let's Play Snap

This activity sees students make suggestions and respond to suggestions. It is inspired by the popular children's card game. Students enjoy the activity and speak lots of English in a short space of time. Prepare a set of picture cards for every two students.*

Method

Students play in pairs, mix the cards and receive half of the cards each. Students do not show their cards to each other. The first player puts a card down face up, looks at the card and makes an appropriate suggestion using, "Let's play badminton," "Let's play tennis," "Let's _____" etc.

---

* The number of cards can vary but I like to use thirty-six cards per set with six different pictures produced six times each and each player starting with eighteen cards.

The next student then puts a card down on top or in a separate pile next to the other player's cards. If the student plays a different card to the previous player, he answers, "Sorry, I can't. I'm tired," "Sorry, I can't. I'm busy," "Sorry I can't. I'm _____" etc. and then makes a new suggestion for the picture on his card. Play continues in the same way until one player puts down the same card. In that situation he replies, "OK/Sure/Sounds good" and picks up all of the cards. He then starts the next round. When one player has no cards left, he loses the game.

Variations

Adapt for different kinds of vocabulary. There are many possibilities. One simple example is to make six different food picture cards six times each and students ask, "Do you like pizza/fish/carrots?" If the other student plays the same food card he answers, "Yes, I do" and collects the cards. If he plays a different food card, he answers, "No, I don't" and plays the next card.

If the class has lots of time and a reasonable level of English, ask students to make their own card sets for a given topic before playing. In this situation it will obviously be more beneficial for their English to write words on the cards instead of drawing pictures.

Rock, Paper, Scissors Knockout

This is a fast moving and fun way to review a lesson or unit of study. It works well with middle-sized classes. No preparation is necessary.

Method

The teacher gives the students a question to be used throughout the game such as, 'What did you do yesterday?' All students stand up at the beginning of the activity and quickly find another student to compete against. If there are an odd number of students standing up, one student pairs off with the teacher. When everyone is ready, one student in each pair asks the question and the other student answers before they swap roles.

After both students have asked and answered they compete in a single round of rock, paper, scissors. The loser must sit down. After all students have finished and the losers have sat down, the winners find a new partner and play continues in exactly the same until the final round. The final round is played as a first-to-three contest to determine the winner.

Variations

When there are an odd number of students left, allow the student without an opponent to choose one of their friends who has already been eliminated back into the game. The two friends then compete against each other. Alternatively, the teacher can choose an eliminated student who is sitting silently and very attentively to come back into the game.

Chain Game (1)

This is a speaking game for practising asking about food. Prepare a card for each student. Each card should have a food written at the top and a different food written at the bottom. There should be five different cards with several students receiving the same card if the class size is large. The number of each card in the set does not necessarily have to be equal. The cards should be made in such a way that they form a complete chain of cards, starting and finishing with the same food e.g. the first card has pizza at the top and ham at the bottom, the second card has ham at the top and sausages at the bottom, the third card has sausages at the top and onions at the bottom, the fourth card has onions at the top and curry at the bottom and the fifth card has curry at the top and pizza at the bottom.

Method

The teacher gives each student a card. Students should not show their card to each other. Students look at their food (at the top of their card) and the food they need to get (at the bottom of their card). Students walk around the classroom and find other students. When a student with pizza at the top of his card and ham at the bottom of his card meets another student, he asks, "I'm hungry. Can I have some ham?" If the other student does not have ham at the top of his card, he answers, "Sorry, I don't have any ham." He does not show his card.

If the student has the right card (ham in this case), he answers, "Sure, here you are," and they stay together for the rest of the game. They then walk around the classroom together and try and find the student with the food at the bottom of the card containing ham at the top. When they find new students, they ask the target question together. Meanwhile, they may get approached by other students in incomplete chains looking for other foods such as a student with curry at the top of his card and pizza at the bottom. When students make a complete chain of five foods, they sit down and attract the attention of the teacher to have their cards checked. The first correctly completed chain wins.

Variations

After the first game, collect all the cards in and replace them with drink cards. Students then walk around saying, "I'm thirsty. Can I have some water/milk/orange juice?" All other aspects of the activity stay the same. If desired, the number of cards in a chain could be changed to four or six.

Down the Line

This is an activity for practising school subjects and asking and answering about a school timetable. Each student needs the same set of six school subject cards, either represented by pictures and/or words. Each subject should be in the set once.

Method

Students play in pairs. Before starting the game, the students practise the subject cards with the teacher. Each student lays a set of six cards face down in a horizontal line across the desk. Students decide who will play first. The first student then has to try and guess the first card of the other player by asking, "Do you have _____ class today?" * The other student looks at his card without

---

* For example, the choices could be art, maths, English, music, science and P.E.

showing his partner. If the first student guesses correctly, the second student answers, "Yes, I do" and turns the card over. The first student must go on to try and guess the second card on his next turn. If the guess is wrong the student answers, "No, I don't." Roles are then reversed regardless of whether the answer was right or wrong. Continue until one player has successfully guessed all of the other player's cards and the whole line has been turned over.

Variations

Changing the number of cards is one possibility but a better adaption is to use the same activity but for a different theme. For example, if the students are studying telephone numbers, make a set of six cards, all with different telephone numbers on and pictures and/or names of people they should be trying to contact. Give the students a set of cards each and a small handout of six telephone numbers. When it is a student's turn he looks at his handout and asks a question such as, "Is that 010-5723-1898?" The other student checks the card and answers, "Yes, it is" or "No, it isn't." Play progresses in the same way as before.

Quiz Games

Quizzes are very versatile and can be adapted and differentiated to the needs of the class. Use them to review topics or units of study. Provide question papers for each student or pair.

Method

Individual or group games are possible but putting students into pairs is recommended. At the end of a unit, make a quiz with about six questions. Put two or three questions on one paper and three questions on another piece of paper. If student levels vary, differentiate the papers and clearly label them or use different coloured paper. Allow each pair to decide between themselves who will do which paper. When the teacher gives a signal, the students turn the papers over and begin.

If one student finishes quickly, he or she may help the other student with any problems but should not do the writing for the student. When a pair finishes, the teacher checks their answer papers and either gives the thumbs up or tells the students how many errors they have made, but not what the mistakes are, to make them read through their answers very carefully one more time. When pairs finish but have one or more incorrect answers, they may change their answers if they are quick enough. Continue until a few pairs successfully complete all questions, generating first place down to third or fifth place. Finally, review the answers together as a class.

Variations

Quizzes which require students to draw the answers instead of writing can be highly motivating. For example if they are studying 'than', problems for them to illustrate could include:

a) Mr Kim's pizza is bigger than Mr Lee's pizza. Mr Lee's pizza is bigger than Mr Ha's pizza.

b) Monkey A's banana is longer than Monkey B's banana.

Adaptations of TV quiz shows can also be very successful. Jeopardy-style games are popular with teachers and students alike. Blockbuster-style games are also a possibility.

5

Games for Upper Intermediate Level Students.

Do It Yourself!

Most students like playing board games. This activity is perfect for an extra-curricular English class when more time can be devoted to big projects. Ideally all of the students in the class will have a reasonably good level although students of slightly lower levels may be successful with some additional support.

Method

Show students various English language board games, preferably including games they have already played. Challenge students to make their own games. They should fill all or some of the game squares on a board with pictures or vocabulary for other students playing the game to read, say the words, construct sentences, or read and do. Students can make games for general English or for a particular topic or sentence structure. Students may also add good or bad squares such as lose a turn, go back to the start or advance on the board. After finishing, students play their new games with their friends.

Variations

Provide some templates for lower level students instead of starting from scratch and/or give them a large selection of options to write or draw on a board and let them choose where to put each item.

The Guessing Sentences Game

This is a game which gives students many chances to practise constructing sentences on a wide variety of subjects. The only preparation required is for the teacher or volunteers to choose a few sentences before starting the game.

Method

The teacher decides whether the game will be played individually or in teams. For larger classes, playing in teams is likely to be better. Next he draws blanks on the whiteboard to indicate the number of words in a sentence. Almost any kind of sentence is suitable including questions as long as the vocabulary and grammar used is within the students' ability range. Shorter sentences usually work better than longer ones.

At the start of the game, the teacher writes the last word of the sentence on to the board or reveals it using something like Microsoft PowerPoint. Students are then asked to guess the whole sentence. For individual games students volunteer to answer, or in a small class the teacher may ask every student to attempt an answer. Students who give the same sentence as the teacher's answer score one point. For team play, give students time to discuss possible answers and choose their final answer. Each team then writes their final answer on to a piece of paper or small board provided by the teacher before the start of the game. Finally, the teacher asks each team to say their answer. Teams score one point for a sentence that is grammatically accurate and able to fit into the blanks and an extra point for giving the same answer that the teacher has. If no team matches the teacher's sentence correctly, the teacher then additionally reveals the penultimate word of the sentence and play continues as before, giving one extra word from the back of the sentence each round until a team gets the correct answer. Continue with further sentences.

Variations

There are several ways to adapt this game. Some students can prepare the game sentences instead of the teacher. The game can be made more difficult by the teacher just revealing one word at a time as before but not the number of words in a sentence. Instead of revealing one word at a time from the back of the sentence, consider doing it from the front. The students will have to guess more, which is not necessarily a bad thing if they are having the chance to practise several sentences for each answer.

Teachers can also consider whether to just give each sentence in isolation or as part of a complete conversation, with the first game sentence being the first thing someone said, the second sentence being the reply and so on.

Take the Answer to the Teacher

This is a game designed to get the students moving and having fun as they practise their English skills. A good topic to use it for is practising listening to and writing down telephone numbers. To prepare, the teacher should write a range of telephone numbers down, prior to the lesson.* Safety is also an important issue to consider in this game. Ensure the classroom layout is suitable for several students to move suddenly in similar directions.†

Method

The students ask the teacher, "What's your telephone number?" and the teacher says a number. The students must write the number down quickly, stand up and take the answer to the teacher as quickly as possible. Students should not take their pencils with them to the teacher. If a student is right he scores a point, earns a sticker or whatever other system the teacher is using. Often the teacher gives the first three correct students a point. If the student has a wrong answer, he must return to his desk and change the answer before returning to the line of students waiting for their answers to be checked. The student

---

* To give the students good real-life examples, some numbers should contain double digits e.g. 010-4499-3992 (oh-one-oh-double four-double nine-three-double nine-two).
† This game is not recommended for smaller or cramped-up classrooms or those where students are sat in long rows.

cannot change his answer while he is standing next to the teacher. In some cases, the teacher may rule that a wrong answer eliminates the student from the rest of the round.

Depending on the ability of the students the teacher may speak very quickly or slightly slower. He may choose to give the students two chances to hear the number by extending the dialogue. After saying the telephone number the first time, the students can then say, "Pardon?" and the teacher repeats the number one more time.

If there are two teachers or adults in the classroom, one can stand in one half of the classroom and the other can stand in the other half, giving students a choice of two places to go, which makes everything fairer. When only one teacher is in the classroom, it is better if he stands in a different part of the classroom for each round so that every student has a chance to start a round in a more favourable place nearer the teacher.

Variations

This game has many other possibilities. It can also be used to practise reading. For instance, the students might ask the teacher, 'Where is the restaurant?' who then reveals directions on a screen or board such as, 'Go straight two blocks, turn right, go straight one block and it is on the left.' Students have to read and then draw the directions, effectively making a small map before taking their answer to a teacher.

The Making Sentences Game

Usually played in teams, this is a good activity for practising listening, reading and sentence construction skills within a unit or topic of study. The teacher needs to decide in advance what sentences to include in the game and then make individual word cards (laminating them if possible) covering all the words that will appear in the game sentences and, quite possibly, a few related words that will not appear in the game. There need to be enough sets of cards for all teams or students. Each set of cards is put in a bag or envelope prior to starting the game.

Method

The teacher gives each team a bag or envelope full of cards. At the start of the game the students put their hands on their heads and wait for the teacher to say a sentence. The teacher can just give a sentence immediately or may choose to make the students participate in a two-way dialogue for a subject relevant to the student's most recent learning. If using dialogues, the teacher gives the last sentence, which is then taken to be the sentence for that round. When the teacher has given the game sentence, the students quickly empty their bag or envelope on to their desks, search for the correct words cards and lay out the sentence the teacher said onto their desk.

When teams begin to finish, they put their hands up or shout their team name and the teacher checks their answers in the order that they finished. It is quite common for teams to make small mistakes such as omitting one word or having at least two words in the wrong place, especially if the sentences are long. If a team makes a mistake, the teacher either simply informs them that they are wrong and leaves the team to try and figure out their mistake, or he may offer a hint as to why they are wrong. If a team gets a wrong answer, they may change their answer immediately but the teacher goes to any other team that has finished, before returning to a team for a second or third time.

The first team to finish correctly scores a point. In a bigger class, the teacher can do a three, two, one point system for first, second and third place. Sentences can be made to be progressively more difficult as the rounds progress. If one team seems to be building up a big lead, the teacher might try to give other teams a chance to make a comeback by offering four or five points for first place on the last one or two questions i.e. the most difficult questions. Scores from each round are added together to find a winner. Be sure to show the students the answer after each round and if applicable, briefly discuss why certain teams had wrong answers, especially in cases where their mistakes were quite minor and not obvious.

Variations

Instead of giving a whole sentence, a teacher can say just one word and then the students have to make a correct sentence, relevant to their unit or topic of study, which uses that word.

5, 4, 3, 2, 1

Students receive a series of clues, which get progressively easier. Students use skill or inspired guesses to score more points. No preparation is essential but some teachers may prefer to make clues in advance.

Method

The teacher thinks of an answer within a chosen topic area and gives the first clue. The clue should be quite difficult. Students or teams then try to guess the right answer. They may only guess once for each clue. If they are right, they score five points. If no-one gets the answer, the teacher gives a slightly easier clue. A right answer from the second clue earns four points, down to one point for the fifth and final clue.

If the students are studying jobs, the answer could be taxi driver with the following clues: He talks to many people (five points), he works outside (four points), he can work in the morning, afternoon or at night (three points), he likes green but hates red (two points) and he works inside a car (one point).

Variations

Force teams to listen and think more and guess less by eliminating them for a wrong answer.

Challenge the higher level students to prepare their own clues and answers for their friends to solve.

Months Game

This is a game that the students enjoy. It can take a long time but the compensation for this is the large amount of English the students will use. Students practise asking, "When is _____?" and answering, "It's in

_____." Students need two dice per pair and a worksheet to check off each answer.*

Method

After practising the game sentences, students pair up (or work in small groups if there are not enough dice to go round) and decide who will play first. Students roll two dice each time and talk about the month that corresponds to the dice score. If a student rolls eight, the other student asks the question on the worksheet for August, the student with the dice answers and then checks August off in his or her column. For example the question might be, 'When is our summer vacation?' and the answer, 'It's in August.' If students roll a number they have already rolled, they do not get any additional credit but they must still practise the question and answer. Play continues in turns.

When a student has checked off every month from February to December (i.e. has rolled every number from two to twelve at least one time), he or she then continues with only one dice each turn until successfully rolling a one for January and answering the question. The other player continues to use two dice if some months from February to

_____

* Make a table covering the months from February to December, with a special day, festival or birthday for each month added. There should be a separate column for each player to check off. There should be a separate section for January. The months should be clearly labelled to avoid confusion.

December have yet to be crossed off in his column. After one player has checked off every month including January, he wins the game.

Variations

Sometimes it can take students a very long time to roll the number they need to get the eleventh and final month they have outstanding between February and December. For time consideration reasons, in some cases the teacher may choose to allow students to cross off their final answer for free immediately after they get their tenth month.

Lower level students can just say the names of the months instead of asking and answering about special days in the months.

Give higher level students a checklist without any events added for each month and ask them to think of and write their own answers before starting the game. They may include some of their friends' birthdays for months in which they cannot think of special days.

Adapt the game for days of the week. Start with one dice for the six days from Sunday to Friday, with students asking, "What day is it today?" and answering, "It's Monday" or "It's Friday." After checking off the first six days students use an extra dice and try to roll seven to win the game.

Beat the Teacher

This activity pits students against their teacher. Students enjoy the thrill of beating the supposedly superior teacher. Prepare large paper and a timer. Books or other aids are optional.

Method

Usually the students play in teams. Choose a time limit and any category for which the students are likely to know lots of vocabulary. When the time starts, students write as many words as possible while the teacher does the same on his paper. All students may write at the same time. Allow students to write in all directions on the paper unless it becomes illegible. When the time is over, check all the answers and the team with the most right words wins.

Variations

Make handicaps to increase the students' chance of winning. Give the students more time than the teacher or challenge the students to get twenty-five answers before the teacher can get fifty. Alternatively, have the same objective for both students and the teacher but allow students access to additional materials such as their study books.

Crazy Chopsticks

In this activity, students ask and answer, "What do you eat for breakfast?" It is a very novel idea for a game, which if organized well, is thoroughly enjoyed by the students. Prepare one pair of chopsticks for each group, small pieces of paper with pictures of breakfast foods on, trays or boxes to put them in and a stopwatch.

Method

The teacher gives each group a small box or tray with pictures of breakfast foods face down and spread out. He also gives each group a pair of chopsticks. The first student in each group takes the chopsticks and the teacher gives ten seconds for the students to conventionally use the chopsticks to pick up answers and put them to one side. It is okay to pick up more than one piece of paper at once. Students should not hold the chopsticks horizontally and scoop several answers out.

When the ten seconds is over, the rest of the students ask, "What do you eat for breakfast?" and the student who used the chopsticks refers to his cards and answers, "I eat bread, cereal, egg, apples, etc.", scoring one point for each right answer. The chopsticks are then passed to the second student, all the pictures are returned face down to their box or tray and the same procedure is followed until every student has tried. After every student has had a turn, either the student with the most points on each table is declared the winner, or if time allows, the winners from each group are gathered and seated together for a championship round. For this, all students play at the same time and the student who picks up the most right answers is declared the winner.

Variations

If the students find it easy to pick up many answers within the ten seconds, increase the time to fifteen seconds but make them use their opposite hand!

For higher level students, put one word on each piece of paper, including some more challenging words related to their recent learning. After they have had their ten seconds with the chopsticks, they score one point for reading each word they picked up and an additional point for making a sentence containing the word.

Teachers that prefer a calmer approach can change the method. Instead of using a timer, students take turns and use the chopsticks to take one answer from the set before continuing with the same question and answer as before (the game can of course be adapted to many different kinds of questions and answers). Papers are not replaced and play continues until every answer has been chosen. If a student cannot make an answer, he does not score the points for that picture. Make the game more interesting by putting a points score from minus one to plus three on each piece of paper. The student with the most points wins the game.

Odd One Out

This can be a wonderful little activity for students of intermediate level and above to practise explaining answers in English. The rich imaginations of children often really shine through in this game. Prepare a couple of example questions before the class.

Method

The teacher introduces the activity with a couple of example questions for the students to attempt to solve, revealing the possible answers one by one. The first question should be very simple to introduce the concept such as choosing the odd one out from cat, dog, tiger and pencil. The second question should offer more possibilities introducing the idea that there is often more than one right answer in this game.*

Students have a few minutes to make their own individual examples before bringing the whole class back together to try answering each other's questions. Allow several guesses per question.

Award one point for a logical and true statement and two points for answering with the same odd one out and same reason as the question setter.

Sometimes students start making questions focussed too much on the alphabet such as one word being the odd one out because it is the only word not containing the letter 'b' or something similar. The teacher may choose to discourage this kind of question.

Variations
Instead of a points system, play only for fun and just reward the one student who made the most interesting or challenging question.

---

* One of my favorites is to show the students pictures of a cucumber, a pepper, a carrot and Shrek. Some students will immediately say Shrek because the others are vegetables but I use the alternative answer of the carrot because the others are green.

Words Rummy

This adaption of the popular playing cards game is for students with quite high ability. Students practise their spelling and word recognition skills. Prepare sets of approximately fifty-two cards with two cards for most letters of the alphabet but make three cards for each vowel and just one for more difficult consonants such as j, q, v, x and z.

Method

Usually between two and four students play each game. Each player receives seven letter cards with the player that will play first receiving an additional card. Students do not show their cards to each other. The remaining cards are placed face down in one pile. Player One must choose one card he does not want and place it face up on the desk. Player Two can then pick up the card put down by Player One, or if that letter card is not useful for making words, he may take the top card off the pack. He then chooses his least useful letter card and places it face up in the same way that Player One did. Play continues until one player can use his seven cards to make one four letter word and one three letter word. Upon revealing the two completed words, he wins the game. Abbreviations are not allowed. Proper nouns may be allowed at the teacher's discretion. If all the cards in the pack get used before a player wins, shuffle the cards on the table and reuse them.

Variations

Add two or more jokers to the pack, which can be used for any letter of the alphabet.

Award a bonus for a student who wins with one seven letter word instead of one four letter and one three letter word.

The O X Game

A common scenario in an English language teaching classroom is for a teacher to play some short footage of a dialogue. Students listen and the teacher then asks a few questions. When the students are enthusiastic, many put their hands up to answer. In other classes, maybe only a handful of students do, even if the teacher plays the footage an additional time. What about the other students? Do we assume they do not know the answers? Or perhaps they are just shy or think they know the answer but are not confident enough to raise their hands. This activity gives all students the chance to show their knowledge.

Prepare large double-sided O, X hand cutouts, two small pieces of paper per student with each piece being a different colour, or any other method of indicating true or false. Alternatively students can make a big O or X with their arms.

Method

After listening to a dialogue, all students stand up. The teacher asks a question and the students have a few seconds to consider their answer. The teacher then counts up to three and all the students show their answer at the same time. After that time they cannot change their answers. If their answer is right, they continue to the next question. If they are wrong, they have to sit down. All students standing after the last question are game winners.

Variations

If possible, create additional chances for students. Consider giving students two lives and taking a card from them after their first wrong answer. If the teacher has a lot of questions, split the game into two shorter games so that students get two opportunities.

Consider choosing a small number of high ability students before showing the dialogue and ask them to listen carefully and set the questions for the rest of the class to answer.

Jigsaw Game

This is an unconventional but enjoyable way for students to practise reading skills and making sentences. Prepare short dialogues within a square or rectangle, cut into jigsaw shaped pieces. Between six and ten pieces is a suitable amount. Prepare envelopes or other suitable objects for storing the pieces before starting a round.*

Method

Students play in teams. Upon the starting signal they empty the pieces on to their desks, look at the words and jigsaw shapes carefully and try to arrange the pieces into a completed puzzle. When students have finished they raise their hands, the teacher checks their answer and if it is correct, asks the team to read the completed dialogue. Award three, two and one points for first, second and third place each round. Add the points to determine the final scores.

Variations

To really challenge students in the last one or two rounds of the game, add some rogue, incorrect or unnecessary pieces to each puzzle set, especially pieces

---

* This game possibly needs the most preparation in this book, especially if a teacher has a large class and needs to make several sets per puzzle. For this reason, laminating all the pieces is highly recommended so the puzzles can be used again later.

containing very similar words or grammar to those that should actually be in the puzzle. Using some homophones is also a good idea.

Relay Game (1)

This is a dynamic fast-paced activity, which involves every team member. It requires good explanation and demonstration before the students play it for the first time but once they understand it they really enjoy it. Prepare identical question card sets for each team, consisting of between six and ten questions. Questions should be related to recent study. To avoid confusion, it is better to use a different colour for each team's cards. It is also better to write the question number on each card. Each team receives paper to write its answers.

Method

Students are divided into teams and numbered depending on the number of questions. Some students may receive two numbers. Question Card One is laid face down on each group's table. The teacher may specify that anyone can write the answers or that students must take it in turns to write the answers. Teams discuss questions and answers as they play. Questions may require teams to write missing words of sentences, one word or whole sentence answers.

Sometimes several answers might be needed for one question, such as 'Write five things you can see on a beach' or 'Write ten past tense words.'

After a team writes an answer, the student whose number matches the question stands up and moves quickly to the teacher's desk, taking the question card and answer paper. Students should not take pens or pencils. If other students go at a similar time, the students must stand in line according to the order they arrived. Only one student per team should be standing up at any one time.

The teacher checks the answer and if it is right, takes the question card and gives the student the next question card and he returns to his team. If the answer is wrong, the teacher returns the card and the student returns to his team. The team then changes its answer before the student goes back to see the teacher. If the answer is wrong, the teacher can simply say, 'Wrong' or offer a hint. If a team cannot answer or does not understand a question, one member of the team goes to the line of students waiting to see the teacher and asks for help.

It is often good to make the last question very challenging or one involving some guess work so that teams may have to try many times to answer it. Another possibility is to make every student in the team go to the teacher together for the last question and sing a song they have learned in the unit of study. Play continues until one team has answered every question. Sometimes play may go on to determine who finishes second or third. At the end of the game review the answers.

Variations

If the students have a low level of English, they can sometimes be asked to draw the answers, instead of writing. For example if they are studying jobs, the question cards may include six policeman, four teachers and five bus drivers. The students read the cards and draw.

If you are team-teaching or have a classroom assistant, it makes the game even more dynamic to have two teacher stations if your classroom is big enough. Make students take odd number questions to one teacher and take even number questions to the teacher on the other side of the classroom. The teachers' desks will need to be carefully set up so that each teacher has the correct cards to give to the students after each right answer. It is also a very wise choice to clearly demonstrate on the whiteboard, which teacher each team needs to go to for which number question. Alternatively, just use one teacher desk and have one teacher walking around and helping any teams having difficulties.

Relay Game (2)

This relay game requires students to work together to write perfect sentences, free of spelling, grammar and punctuation errors. Students need chalk or board markers.

Method

A number of students are divided into two equal sized teams, with each team member lined up one behind the other a few metres away from the board. Each team uses one side of the board. At the start of the game the teacher gives a sentence related to the students' recent learning. The number of words in the sentence should match the number of students in a team.

After hearing the sentence, the first student runs to the blackboard and quickly writes the first word on the board. The student then runs back and passes the chalk to the second student. The new student writes the second word, continuing for all the members of the team. If any student spots a mistake by any previous member of the team, he may change the mistake, using a board eraser if necessary, as well as writing his own word but he may never write the next student's word. If a team spots a mistake (including very small ones such as no full stop) after every word has been written, any team member may go and change it.

Unless one team is particularly slow, continue until both teams think they have the right answer. Then ask the students who did not participate in the current round whether the sentences are right or not and if they are incorrect, ask why they are wrong. If both teams are right, the fastest team to finish wins the round. When one or both teams have finished the teacher may tell them how many mistakes they have made if any, or he can just leave the teams to figure it out for themselves.

Variations

If the students have reasonably good ability, give them chance to be more creative by not giving them a sentence. Use the same format of one word per student but instead they have to make their own sentences on any subject by reading the words written by the previous members of their team and writing a word that continues the sentence naturally and in a grammatically correct form. If slightly more structure is required, follow the above method but give them a sentence subject. If the subject is fruit and there are five team members, the first student could write, 'I', the second student, 'like', third student, 'apples', fourth student, 'and' and the fifth student, 'oranges.'

The game can be changed into a reading activity with similarities to The Making Sentences Game (see page 111).

The teacher attaches several word cards all over the board, with the same set of cards for each team. The teacher reads a sentence and students go to the board one by one in the same way as above and move one card each until they have a correct sentence. Students could again also make sentences of their own in the same way as described above.

The Argument Game

This is a fun activity for practising sentences with the word 'than'. Students are often inspired to think of and attempt more sentences in their bid for supremacy. For alternative versions, prepare small picture cards of famous people.

Method

Two students are chosen to play at one time. After the first student has been chosen, he or she must make a sentence, speaking in a firm voice, using the structure, "I'm _____ than you." Students can talk about appearance, abilities or anything else they can think of. Avoid allowing students to use sentences with the structure, "You're _____ than me," as the answers could get negative and upset students. After the first student successfully makes a sentence, the other student must make a retort. Play continues back and forth until a student says a sentence that is clearly not true such as, 'I'm taller than you,' to a taller student, repeats an answer or better still is rendered speechless after a lengthy argument.

Variations

Instead of playing the game on a personal level, ask each student to randomly take a picture of a famous person and show it to the class. Students then put themselves in the shoes of the famous people and the argument commences!

Dictionary Race

An often totally neglected area of study, the ability to find words quickly in an English dictionary, is a useful skill. Students can read meanings and practise their spelling. You will need at least two dictionaries (preferably identical) or one dictionary plus a timer. Consider using picture dictionaries for very young students.

Method

If only one dictionary is available, choose students one by one and time them. If there are more dictionaries, chosen students search for the target word at the same time.

Most commonly, a teacher or volunteer chooses a word that the students are likely to know and students try to find the word as quickly as possible. When the student finds the word, the teacher checks it is the right word. Depending on the level of the students, the teacher may ask the student to read the definition of the word as soon as he or she finds it. The fastest student wins the round. After a word has been found, ask all students to spell the word. This can be done before searching instead if preferred.

Variations

Choose words in advance, give volunteers the word each side of the target word in the dictionary and ask them to find the word in the middle. Also give the other students the chance to predict the middle word in advance.

Alphabet Challenge

This activity practises vocabulary within a particular category. It is a simple concept but often provides a substantial challenge and is generally enjoyed by students.

Method

It is possible to play individually, but usually this activity is attempted in small groups. Students are given a category and then challenged to find one answer for each letter of the alphabet. Often X and Y are put together as one. Countries and jobs are two particularly good subjects for this game. Play continues until one team has a complete alphabet of correct answers or until a specified time limit expires, in which case the team with the most right answers wins. Right answers but wrong spellings are acceptable at the teacher's discretion and taking the level of the students into consideration.

Variations

Offering teams the possibility to 'buy' help at the cost of a small number of points adds an interesting dimension to this game. Depending on the resources available in the classroom, help may come in the form of access to books or the internet for a small period of time. By using other resources, students initially lose points but take the risk that they will find enough answers to finish with more points in the long run.

The game can also be differentiated by giving lower level students some of the answers before starting, especially for a selection of the more difficult letters.

Yes/No Game

This is an activity that really makes the students think about the type of questions they ask.

Method

The teacher or a volunteer thinks of a word in a particular category such as animals. At the start of the game the teacher specifies the number of questions and guesses allowed in a bid to get the right answer. Generally, ten questions and five guesses work well. Students or teams must try to work out the word by asking questions that can only be answered with, 'Yes' or 'No'. If they ask a question that cannot be answered with, 'Yes' or 'No', they lose the question from their total of available questions. Play continues until someone answers correctly or until all available questions and guesses have been used up without saying the correct answer.

Variations

The game can be made significantly more challenging by only allowing one attempt at the final answer, resulting in a win or bust outcome.

Tongue Twisters

This is a fun way to make the students speak English. Depending on the choice of tongue twisters the activity can be linked to the study of past tense.[*]

Method

The teacher gives students one or more tongue twisters to practise. 'Peter Piper picked a peck of pickled peppers' is always a good one to use, as is, 'Silly Sally sliced some sizzling sausages.' There are numerous other possibilities.

There are a few methods of playing. If students play individually, the teacher either checks how many times the student can successfully say the tongue twister within a time limit or times how long it takes to say the tongue twister a set number of times. If playing in teams, students take it in turns to say the tongue twister when it is their turn to take the challenge.

---

[*] If students need extra motivation or encouragement, ask them to teach you a tongue twister from their own language. The sight and sound of their teacher fumbling hopelessly, either deliberately or otherwise, is likely to generate a few laughs and also reduce any inhibitions students may have. If you are teaching in South Korea, students will probably enjoy teaching you the tongue twister, '간장공장 공장장은 장공장장이고 된장공장 공장장은 강공장장이다'

Variations

Give the students an opportunity to make their own tongue twisters and then choose the best ones for the whole class to attempt.

Where Are You From?

Students are very interested in learning how to say countries in English. This game builds on that. It works better for higher ability classes.

Method

Each student, pair or small group receives a piece of paper. The teacher then invites students to write a list of countries in English on their papers within a time limit.

After writing, the teacher chooses a student or group to start and instructs all the other groups to ask together, "Where are you from?" The chosen student or group must then say, "I'm from _____" and add one of the countries from their paper. Any group that has that country marks it on their paper and earns one point. Play continues until every student or team has given one answer. At the end of the game, each player or team counts up the number of countries they marked off and whoever has most points wins the game.

Variations

Play individually and ask every student to write one country. All students stand up. Students ask the teacher together, "Where are you from?" and the teacher gives an answer. Anyone who has the teacher's answer must sit down. Repeat until only one student is left standing.

6

Games for All.

3, 6, 9

3, 6, 9 is a fun activity based on a popular Korean game, adapted for use in English classrooms. It is suitable for both large and small classes. No preparation is necessary for this game.

Method

After selecting an order of play, students start counting from one, saying just one number each per turn. If a number contains a three, six, or nine (not necessarily multiples of three), a student must clap once instead of saying a number. If a number contains two threes, sixes or nines (e.g. thirty-three or thirty-six) then the student whose turn it is, must clap twice.

If a student says a number instead of clapping, claps instead of saying a number, claps the wrong number of times, says a number out of sequence or cannot answer within a reasonable time he is eliminated from the game and play resumes from the next student, going back to one again. The game continues until only one student remains. The game works well whether students are standing up or sitting down.

The correct sequence goes as follows: one, two, clap, four, five, clap, seven, eight, clap, ten, eleven, twelve, clap, fourteen, fifteen, clap, seventeen, eighteen, clap, twenty, twenty-one, twenty-two, clap, twenty-four, twenty-five, clap, twenty-seven, twenty-eight, clap, clap, clap, clap, clap two times, clap, clap, clap two times, clap, clap, clap two times, forty, forty-one, forty-two, clap, forty-four, forty-five, clap, forty-seven, forty-eight, clap, fifty and so on.

Variations

For students who can count well, repeat the method above but instead of going up in ones, go up in tens or hundreds.

For students who already know the game method, the game could be adapted for ordinal numbers (first, second, clap, fourth, fifth, clap, seventh, eighth, clap, ten ... twenty-seventh, twenty-eighth, clap, clap, clap, clap, clap two times, clap, clap, clap two times, clap, clap, clap two times, fortieth etc.)

One nice alternative can be used when studying the time. The teacher gives students a starting time and an increase in minutes each time with students being required to clap every time the time comes round to o'clock. For example if the teacher gave a starting time of 6:40 and an instruction of plus ten minutes, play would continue as follows: 6:40, 6:50, clap, 7:10, 7:20, 7:30, 7:40, 7:50, clap,

8:10. When a student is eliminated the teacher chooses a new starting time and play continues from the next student.

Fill the Board

This simple activity is good for practising vocabulary or grammar within a particular category. No preparation is essential although the teacher may wish to prepare a selection of bonus answers in advance.

Method

The teacher selects a category related to what the students have studied and challenges the students to fill the whiteboard with as many answers as possible. The teacher writes all the answers on the board. Students may be asked to say all the sport, food or family words they know or the teacher may turn it into a general vocabulary game and write one letter on the board and ask students to say all the words they know starting with that particular letter. A grammar focus is also possible with students saying only past tense or present continuous verbs for example. Students are not usually permitted to look at their books. Play continues until the students' answers totally fill the board or until there is no more time left.

Variations

The challenge and satisfaction of successfully filling the teacher's board will be enough for many students. If more motivation is needed, do the same task for other classes and invite each class to try and get the highest score in the school.

Preparing special hidden or bonus words before the class is often popular, with the students receiving a point or other reward if their answers are revealed at the end of the game. If the teacher has a good relationship with the class, he or she could add an amusing twist by also preparing a small number of penalty words, which have negative consequences of some sort.

Last Man Standing

This repetitive drilling style activity is both fast moving and popular with students. This activity is ideal for practising days of the week.

Method

All students stand in a line at the start of the game. Play starts with a student at one end of the line. The first student says, "Sunday" and then the following students must say the next day in sequence each time. If a student says the wrong day or hesitates for too long, he is out and must sit out for the rest of the game. Play then continues from the next student, going back to Sunday again.

Variations

Practising months rather than days works well. Using it to practise counting is also effective whether it be going up by one, two, three or in bigger steps such as tens. Revert to the first number after each wrong answer.

Apple-Elephant

This is an easy game that English learners can play even from a very early stage of English acquisition. It is good for practising words, learning some new words and helping students' spelling.

Method

The teacher writes a word on the board. Students or teams then take it in turn to make the new word. Each proceeding word must begin with the last letter of the preceding word. If a team or student cannot make a word or says a word that has already been used, they are out, score minus one point or plus one point is awarded to the player who gave the previous word. Play then continues with the same letter for the next player or team. If all teams are unable to make a word for a particular letter, the teacher may give an answer to get the game moving again. Plurals are not allowed but the teacher may choose to allow some proper nouns.[*]

Variations

Instead of just deciding the winner by who can make the most words, play a race to one hundred points. Every time a team says a word, the number of letters in their word are counted and added to their total until there is a winner.[†]

Slam Game

This is a game which requires the students to combine their English listening skills with lightning reflexes. The activity generally generates a lot of excitement.

Method

Each pair or group receives a set of cards, which they lay out over the desk face up. Cards may be picture or word cards depending on the topic, ability of the students and the

---

[*] I allow the names of countries, cities and days of the week.
[†] Beware of the smart student who suddenly says, "Supercalifragilisticexpialidocious!" Do not get caught out like I did by one class. Ban the word or learn the spelling!

145

skill the teacher is focusing on. Before each answer, the students put their hands on their heads.

At the teacher's signal, the students ask the teacher a question and then listen to the response. For example, the students might ask, 'What did you do in the summer vacation?' and the teacher answers, 'I practised the piano.' The students then have to slam a hand down on the right card. They may not change their answer, or hover their hands around over the cards before slamming an answer. A hand must go straight down in a brisk, smooth motion. After a student gets a right answer he keeps the card and play continues until no cards remain. Alternatively the cards are not collected but students score one point per right answer. In this version, the same answers can be used more than once with play continuing for a few minutes.

Variations

Instead of playing small games sat at desks, make students stand up, spread cards all around the classroom and make a big team game.

Another possibility is to test students reading skills by making cards with similarly spelt words.

There is also a similar game called, 'Snatch,' which sees the students aim to snatch the cards off the desk before other students.

Act Out the Card

This is a fairly simple, fun, kinesthetic game to review vocabulary within one or more categories. The teacher usually prepares picture cards. If word cards are used instead, students can also practise basic reading.

Method

Students stand up. All but two students stand together, facing the same direction. Another student within the team stands behind those students, facing the same way. The remaining student stands away from the other students but facing them. When the teacher gives the cue, the student behind the other students briefly holds up a picture or word card and the student facing the others looks at the card and then has to act the picture or word out, without speaking. The other students have to guess what the actions mean.

Unless the teacher specifies otherwise, the students may continue guessing after wrong answers until they say the right answer. When they give a right answer, they score one point and play continues until the time runs out. The team which scores the most points wins the game. The game can be played with the same student from a team always doing the actions or students can change over quickly after each right answer.

Variations

Challenge higher level students by giving them short sentences to act out, rather than words. Alternatively they can be asked to describe the word without actually saying it.

Simon Says

This is a fun game, suitable for most ability levels and can be played to practise or review work (i.e. just for fun, without elimination) or it can be played competitively.

Method

If the teacher gives a command, "Simon says _____," the students must follow the command. If the teacher gives a command without saying, 'Simon says' first, the students should ignore it. If students ignore a 'Simon says' command, respond to a command without 'Simon says', cannot understand, are too slow or their actions do not match the command, they are knocked out.

For very low level students instructions might include stand up, clap your hands, sit down, jump etc. More complex orders can be given to more able students.

Variations

Directions are a good topic for this game. In addition to the ways outlined above for eliminating students, students are likely to get left and right mixed up.

Alphabet Chocolate Game

South Korea has some bags of chocolates called, 'ABC' in which, chocolates have a letter of the alphabet carved into the middle. Teachers in other countries might have to improvise e.g. wrapping letter papers around regular chocolate wrappers.

Method

The teacher pulls a chocolate from the packet and says the letter. The first student to shout out a word with that letter wins the chocolate. If the class is quite big, the teacher might ask students to put their hand up as soon as they think of an answer. Alternatively each round can be restricted to one group or only boys etc. For low level students or beginners to English, any word with the chosen letter should suffice. Higher level students can be asked to give an answer within a category e.g. seasons.

Variations

Ask more able students to give two or more words within a category to win the chocolate or make them use the chosen letter as the second or last letter of their answers.

Survey Game

This is a highly productive activity, where students are given one or more questions to investigate. Students are usually extremely motivated to ask as many other students as possible. Prepare answer sheets beforehand.

Method

The teacher gives students a worksheet with one or more questions to investigate. Closed questions generally work best. The most common method is to have one question structure such as, 'Can you _____?' or 'Do you like _____?' and a range of activities or foods to explore e.g. Can you play baseball? Can you play the piano? Can you dance?

After practising the questions and possible answers, the teacher asks the students to stand up, walk around, meet and ask their friends and then record their findings, usually using a simple format such as O and X. Students continue until they have filled up their sheet, asked a specified number of students or the allocated time runs out.

Variations

Instead of asking all or a set number of children, the students can be asked to continue until they find and record a certain number of students with the same answer. For example they could be asked to find and record five students who like strawberries or ten students who can swim.

Higher or Lower?

This is a simple, fun and fast moving number game, which is not only suitable for students of most ability levels but also a game where the higher level students are unlikely to have any significant advantage. Prepare number or price cards beforehand.

Method

Depending on what the students already know or have studied in recent lessons, the activity might be based around, 'How much is it?' whereby the students attempt to guess the price of something (usually a fictional price chosen by the teacher or a student), 'How old is _____?', giving the students the chance to guess the age of someone they know or someone whose photo they are shown, or just simply guess the number hidden on a card or piece of paper. The better the students, the higher the answers can go.

At the beginning of the game, one student takes a guess at the answer and the teacher or volunteer with the answer responds with, 'Higher' or 'Lower'. Play continues in the same way with another student guessing the answer and carries on until a student finally says the correct answer.

Variations

This activity can also be used in the same way for ordinal numbers, either trying to guess someone's birthday date (limited to 31st) or with no restrictions.

A guess the year game is also possible. Show pictures or old TV clips and guess or show a picture of a famous person (dead or living) and ask when that person was born. Students could also guess the years of inventions.

1, 2, 3, 4, 5

This is an activity bearing some resemblance to bingo, with a points system that keeps everyone interested until the very end. Teachers should prepare a game handout on A4 or A5 paper, containing the target question five times. For each question, there are two possible answers, which can be represented by words or pictures. Put a box next to each question to record the points.

Method

Each student receives a handout and quickly circles one of the two answers for each question. When everyone is ready, the teacher gives a signal and all of the students ask the target question in a big voice e.g. 'What do you want to do?' The teacher then gives one of the two answers on the worksheet e.g. 'I want to play the piano.' Students who circle the same answer before the game that the teacher subsequently gives, score one point for question one. Repeat for questions two to five. Students score two points for a right answer on question two, three points for question three, four points for question four and five points for question five making a maximum of fifteen points. All wrong answers score zero. The student with the most points wins.

Variations

Another possibility is to give the students three answers to choose from for each question or to have two possible answers for the first four questions and three possible answers just for the last question, i.e. the question that has the most points at stake. The number of questions could also be increased, for example making a 1, 2, 3, 4, 5, 6, 7 game. Almost any alternative question and selection of answers can be used too.

Memory Game (5)

This is a simple game in which students say many different words either generally, or within a category. The game is suitable for all ability levels.

Method

The game can be played individually or in teams depending on the size of the class and whether the teacher wants a whole class game or private group games.

The first team or student says a word and then the next team or student must repeat the first answer and then give an additional answer. The third team or student must say the first two answers in the correct order and then add another answer. A new answer is added each time. If an answer is repeated, said out of sequence or no additional answer is given then the person or team involved is either eliminated or scores minus one point.

A simple method is for the first student to say a word beginning with 'a' and the second student continuing with a 'b' word and so on.

Variations

Challenge higher level students by asking them to only answer with seasonal words, toys, sports, action verbs etc. Category based games are not usually done alphabetically.

Bingo

This is possibly the most popular game in the teaching of foreign languages. Almost all students love bingo and it can be used for all ability levels. It can be used for reviewing vocabulary or practising questions and replies.

Method

Assuming students will make their own bingo game grids, the teacher gives a category and tells students to quickly write their answers into a grid. Many students will need a range of possible answers to refer to. A three by three grid is the most common. For students who cannot write well, the teacher may ask them to quickly draw instead of writing the answers. The vocabulary can cover any topic from letters of the alphabet to whole sentence answers to a question.

When the students are all relatively new to English, the teacher may just say words and the students check the answers off. For higher level classes, the students often ask a target question such as, 'What time is it?' and the teacher or individual students give an answer. Play usually continues until students have a predetermined number of lines or a full house.

Variations

Double the amount of times the students use the vocabulary by making them ask the teacher the target question several times before the game and then randomly put the teacher's answers into their grids each time. For example if students ask, 'How old are you?' the teacher gives a different answer each time and notes them down, ready to use the same answers later. All students end up with the same answers but in different squares of their grids. When the students have filled their grids, the game begins, following the normal game procedure.

Add extra twists to the game by giving bonus opportunities. Before particular turns in the game, announce that any student who has the next answer in the centre or a nominated corner of their bingo grid will receive a bonus point, sticker, candy or other perk depending on the systems in use in the classroom.

Olympic Relay

This is a good activity anytime but even more so if some of the students have seen the Olympics or a big athletics meeting on television recently. Students practise counting from one to a hundred. Prepare a stopwatch or other timer. A baton or equivalent is an optional extra.

Method

Students are usually put into teams of four. Each team plays separately. The four students spread out around the classroom, starting in the four corners of the classroom. The first student receives a baton of some sort, or simply ask the students to tap hands instead.

When the teacher starts the timer, the first student counts from 1-25 as quickly as possible and then runs to the second student and passes on the baton. Continue with the second student counting from 26-50, the third student from 51-75 and the final student from 76-100. When the final student runs to and reaches the starting point, the teacher stops the timer. Repeat for the other teams. The fastest team wins.

Variations

Count in tens up to one thousand, hundreds up to ten thousand or whatever other steps and totals the teacher feels will challenge the students.

Give each team a country team name to motivate it and generate an Olympic feeling. Who will win the gold, silver and bronze medals?

Flicking Games

This is an interesting alternative to a regular board game, requiring students to combine their English ability with dexterity skills. Prepare coins, erasers or other objects that can be flicked. Make boards containing a number of squares. Each area should be filled with a picture, word or sentence related to the students' study topic.

Method

Students are divided into pairs and receive a board and something to flick. Students take it in turn to flick. Students usually flick from the same starting point each turn. If they land off the board, they lose their turn.

When a student lands on a square he looks at the contents and makes a sentence. If the students have been studying time and land on a square which says 'homework', an answer might be, 'I do my homework at five o'clock.' The square is then marked in some way. The other player may still land on the square. Continue in turns until one player has landed on every square or there is no time left, at which point the player who has marked the most squares wins the game.

Variations

Add interesting twists such as a Santa Claus square, which allow the students to mark off one or more of the more difficult to reach squares free. Add a crocodile square, which will 'eat' the students and erase all of their right answers!

Noughts and Crosses

This is a very simple, fun and fast-moving way of practising any target language.

Method

Students pair up, draw a three by three grid and decide who will use O and who will use X. The teacher gives the students a dialogue to use each time. For example the dialogue might be, 'Do you want a fork?' followed by, 'Yes, please/No, thanks. I can use chopsticks.'

Students say the dialogue and then finish with a round of rock, paper, scissors. The winner puts an O or X into the grid and then students swap roles with the student who answered, asking and the student who asked, answering. Students continue swapping roles each time until one student has three in a line.

Variations

Use four by four or five by five grids and either the student who makes the most lines of three or the student who gets the most squares wins.

Guess the Song

This game is likely to work best after the teacher has been teaching a class for several months or longer and has taught the students a significant number of English songs. You will need a musical instrument or internet equivalent[*] and knowledge of the music to various English songs, or music sheets to read from. Review all of the potential songs in advance, to decide how many notes offers a challenge without being virtually impossible.

---

[*] A simple but sufficient on-line keyboard can be found at: http://www.primaryresources.co.uk/music/piano.html

Method

The students usually play in teams. The teacher or a student volunteer randomly chooses a song from the available songs* and plays the first few notes (usually between three and five). The students then have a little thinking time to discuss and write down an answer. If a team is right, it scores a point. If no team answers correctly, play another two or three notes and finally two or three more notes. If no team can answer successfully after the three hints, reveal the answer and play a longer section of the song.

Often the students will know the tune but will not know the accurate title so if their answer reflects that they clearly do know the song, show plenty of leniency e.g. allow 'Little Star' if the song is 'Twinkle Twinkle Little Star'.

After one or more teams answer correctly, ask all of the students to sing the song with an enthusiastic voice. Some teachers may choose to award a bonus point for the team or teams that sing the song the best.

---

* Use a selection of the best and easiest songs from the student's current and recent study books as well as classic childrens' English songs such as Old MacDonald, Twinkle Twinkle Little Star, B.I.N.G.O. and alphabet songs.

Variations

One possibility is to modify the points system, giving three points if a team gets the answer after the first hint, two points after the second and three points after the last hint.

If the students are going to study a well-known pop song, this activity is one way to introduce the song, although a greater number of notes than normal may be necessary.

Drawing Race Game

This is a fast moving activity to test the students' listening skills. It can be used to practise prepositions or shapes and colours. It works better in small classes. Provide the students with chalk or board markers.

Method

The teacher divides the blackboard or whiteboard into a few sections, one for each student participating in a round. The teacher or student volunteer gives a sentence containing a preposition such as, 'The bird is on the cat's head' or 'The bird is in the cat's stomach' and each student must draw an accurate picture as quickly as possible. Remind students they are being judged on their accuracy and not the quality of their picture. Allow enough time for most students to finish and then ask the rest of the class to judge whether the pictures match the sentence. The student who finished quickest with an accurate picture is the winner of the round. Choose new students for a new round.

Variations

Use this activity for low level students when they are studying shapes. Give them a command containing a sequence of shapes such as, 'Star, triangle, square, circle' and the first student to finish correctly wins again. If you have coloured chalk, challenge the students more with commands such as, 'Red circle, blue square, white circle, blue triangle'.

If the class size is large, give every student a piece of paper and they draw their answers and hold the paper up as soon as they have finished.

Four Corners

This is a dynamic, fast-moving, kinesthetic game, enjoyed by almost all students. It is used for practising a question and answer for a given topic. You should label each of the four corners of the classroom. You will need a blindfold and depending on the classroom it may be necessary to rearrange furniture.[*]

Method

At the start of the game, the teacher reveals the game question and allocates an answer to each of the four corners of the classroom. For example the question could be, 'When is your birthday?' with corner answers of, 'It's in January/February/March/April.' [†] One student is blindfolded and stands in the middle of the classroom.

In the first round, the teacher counts down briskly from ten to zero and each student rushes to a corner. If any student tries to communicate with the blindfolded student, he or she is immediately out of the game. After counting down to zero, students cannot change their corner. The teacher asks the game question and the blindfolded student answers. The students standing in the corner matching the answer are out and must sit down. Choose an 'out' student to take the blindfold for the next round with the blindfolded student from the first round joining in the game. From the second round onwards ask the students who have been

---

[*] Students need to be able to move around easily and quickly. A big classroom is ideal for this game. Some classrooms will be too small or unsuitable in other ways.

[†] There are many other possibilities including, 'Where is X?', 'He/She is in the living room/kitchen/bathroom/bedroom' (draw a house on the board for emphasis) or, 'Where are you from?', 'I'm from England/France/Germany/Italy.'

eliminated to do the countdown from ten to zero and to ask the game question in a big voice instead of the teacher. Continue, choosing a new student to be blindfolded each round, until there is only one student left in the game or no time remaining.

To ensure the game's excitement, each game should be fast-moving throughout and finish quite quickly. The teacher should ensure quick transitions of only a few seconds between rounds. This also ensures that students that have already been eliminated remain focused.

After one game, students will want to play again, so change the vocabulary before starting a new game. For example, if the game question is about birthdays, change answers to the next four months of the year. If the game question is about countries, choose four new countries.

Variations

Students usually only have one chance in this game. However, to ensure participation from the eliminated students throughout, it is sometimes a good idea for the first few rounds to allow one of the sitting down students back into the game per round. After the countdown from ten to zero, choose the student who asks the target question in the most enthusiastic voice.

Index

About the author

Adrian Bozon is a qualified England primary school teacher. He has also taught English as a foreign language to students of all ages, most notably for several years in a South Korean elementary school. He has taught students of all ability levels in small, medium and large class sizes. He has taught in various teaching environments including extensive experience of team-teaching in addition to regular solo-teaching. Adrian has also worked closely with over two hundred Korean student teachers.

Also by Adrian Bozon

100 Great EFL Quizzes, Puzzles and Challenges: Stimulating, Photocopiable, Language Activities for Teaching English to Children and Young Learners of ESL and EFL.

ISBN 978-0956796813

Lightning Source UK Ltd.
Milton Keynes UK
UKOW031851010413

208498UK00013B/222/P